ROMANIA

- tourist guide -

text
MARIANA PASCARU

photographs
FLORIN ANDREESCU

text
MARIANA PASCARU

photographs
FLORIN ANDREESCU

design
RADU DAVID

english translation
ALISTAIR BLYTH

academic consultants
ANA DOBJANSCHI (History of Art)

image processing
GINA BÜLL

maps
© CARTOGRAPHIA LTD. BUDAPEST, 2007

Descrierea CIP a Bibliotecii Naționale a României
ANDREESCU FLORIN
Romania: tourist guide / foto: Florin Andreescu; text: Mariana Pascaru
trad. lb. eng.: Alistair Blyth - București; Ad Libri, 2007
ISBN 978-973-7887-60-3
913(498)(036)

Published © AD LIBRI
tel./fax: 021-212.35.67, 021-210.88.64; tel: 021-610.37.92;
e-mail: adlibri@b.astral.ro
www.adlibri.ro

The publisher endeavours to provide readers with complete and up-to-date factual information. We are nevertheless aware that, between the date this guide is published and that in which it is purchased, various modifications may appear in the information offered herein. We apologise for any eventual oversights and shall be grateful to all those who point them out. Any other observations or new information regarding the subject matter of the guide will be regarded as welcome.

The Rucăr-Bran corridor, winter

Romania – general information

Romania is situated in Southeast Europe. Its natural boundaries are the Danube River in the south, the Prut River in the east, and the Tisa River in the north (for a small section). Romania borders Ukraine and the Republic of Moldova in the east and north, Hungary in the west and north-west, Serbia in the south-west and Bulgaria in the south.

Surface area: 238,391 square kilometres

Population: 21,733,556 inhabitants (2003), of which 89% are Romanians. The largest minorities are Hungarians and Szeklers (7.1%), and Roma (1.7%).

Official language: Romanian

Form of government: republic

Main religion: Orthodox Christianity (86.8% of the population). Other Christian denominations: Roman Catholic (5%), Graeco-Catholic (Uniate) (1%), Protestant (3.5%)

National flag: red, yellow and blue, in vertical bands, with blue next to the flagpole

Capital: the Municipality of Bucharest (2,064,000 inhabitants), situated in the south-east of the country, on the Walachian Plain, on the banks of the Dâmbovița and Colentina rivers; first attested in 1459

Other major cities: Timișoara, Iași, Constanța, Brașov, Cluj-Napoca, Oradea

Official time: GMT + 3 hours during summer (from the last Sunday in March until the last Sunday in October) and GMT + 2 hours during the rest of the year

Climate: temperate-continental. The average temperature in summer is 22-24 degrees Celsius, but maximum temperatures may even reach 38 degrees Celsius. In the winter, the average temperature is below minus 3 degrees Celsius.

National currency: the LEU. 1 leu = 100 bani. Banknotes in circulation: 1, 5, 10, 50, 100 and 500 lei. Coins in circulation: 1, 5, 10 and 50 bani. Currency exchange: at banks and at currency exchange bureaux, which can be found in hotels, airports and train stations, in supermarkets and on main urban thoroughfares. It is advisable not to change money on the black market, in order to avoid being cheated. Credit cards: large hotels, restaurants and supermarkets usually accept American Express, MasterCard, Diner's Club, and Visa. Payment by credit card is becoming ever more widespread.

Telephone prefixes for Romania: country code – 0040; Bucharest – 021 (when dialling from outside the capital) or 21 (when dialling from abroad).

Emergency telephones: 112 (for emergency services anywhere within the country).

Official holidays: 1 December – National Day of Romania; 1 and 2 January – New Year; 1 May – Labour Day; the first and second days of Easter; 25 and 26 December – Christmas.

Unirii Boulevard, Bucharest

Romania – the natural setting

In Romania, the traveller will have no opportunity to get bored – and we can say so without any risk of exaggeration. Not infrequently reckoned a "country of paradoxes", Romania cannot fail to stimulate our interest. The curious fact has often been remarked that this is a Latin nation in the midst of Slav and Ugric peoples. It is a majority Orthodox country, with a name that nevertheless preserves the memory of Rome... Romania is situated at the "gates of the Orient", but is nevertheless a western country in very many respects.

Although it has a surface area of just under 240,000 square kilometres, Romania can boast almost all forms of geographical relief: mountains, sea, delta, lakes, hills, winding valleys, caves, gorges, waterfalls...

Tourists are particularly fascinated by the course of the *Danube* through Romania. For 1,075 kilometres, the ancient River Danubius provides fabulous vistas. Along the banks of the Danube, sub-Mediterranean vegetation has developed (in spite of the fact that we find ourselves in a zone of continental climatic influence) and mysterious karst formations can be found. The *Cauldrons* 144 km section of the *Danube Gorges* is not to be missed.

Before it empties into the Black Sea, the Danube splits into three long branches (Chilia, Sulina and Saint George), between which has formed a wild delta. At not more than ten thousand years old, this is the youngest terrain in the country. A "paradise" for all kinds of plants and wild animals, the Danube Delta has been made an UNESCO world biosphere reservation.

Romania has the rare advantage of an opening onto the Black Sea, with a coastline of approximately 240 kilometres. Along the coast, there is a chain of wonderful resorts: Mamaia, Năvodari, Eforie Nord, Eforie Sud, Costinești, Olimp, Neptun, Jupiter, Venus, Saturn, Mangalia, Vama Veche. Constanța, built on the ruins of the ancient Greek colony of *Tomis* – the famous site of Latin poet Ovid's exile – is Romania's most important Black Sea port.

More than half the length of the Carpathian Mountains, which are part of the Alpine-Carpathian-Himalayan chain, is to be found on the territory of Romania. The Romanian Carpathians are a paradise for skiers, hikers and extreme-sports enthusiasts. Here, there is snow cover for between 100 and 120 days a year. In the mountains, there are numerous marked routes, with varying degrees of difficulty. The

View towards the Bucegi Mountains

most accessible mountain resorts are in the Prahova Valley, flanked by the *Bucegi* and *Baiului Mountains: Sinaia*, the former residence of the royal family, *Bușteni, Azuga, Predeal*. The *Făgăraș Massif* holds the record for altitude, with its apparently unassailable Moldoveanu peak (2,544m). *Piatra Craiului* is a crest of grey-white limestone, with high walls, rocky shelves, crags and scree. The "stone citadel" of the *Apuseni Mountains* is a realm of karst phenomena: the Ponor Forts, the Living Flame Glacier, the Padiș Plateau, the Galbena Gorges, the Warm Someș, the Râmeți. The *Retezat Massif*, with its eighty glacial tarns (Bucura, Zănoaga, Black Tarn, Ana, Lia, Viorica), is home to a national park of 54,400 hectares, and has been declared a Biosphere Reservation. The *Maramureș Mountains* are traversed by the Vaser Valley, along the length of which runs an archaic narrow gauge steam railway. In Gutâi, one is particularly struck by the Cockerel Crest – a sheer wall of volcanic rock with an altitude of 1,438 metres. The *Rodnei Mountains* preserve numerous glacial traces: crests, valleys, morains. We cannot speak of the *Rarău Massif* without mentioning the mysterious Lady's Rocks. On the plateau of the *Căliman Mountains*, of volcanic origin, there tower the *Twelve Apostles Rocks*, which seem to transport us to the mythic beginnings of the world.

The Carpathian Mountains have been likened to a "stronghold of waters". For it is here that hundreds of rivers and streams begin their journey through Romania, representing ninety-eight per cent of the country's hydrographic network: the *Olt, Mureș, Ialomița, Someș, Argeș, Siret, Jiu, Râmeț*. The course of these waters through the Romanian mountains sometimes becomes a veritable spectacle. The *Nerei, Turda, Bistrița, Oltețului, Runcului (Sohodolui), Bicazului*, and *Tătarului* are just some of the country's two hundred gorges.

Subterranean Romania conceals approximately twelve thousand caves, whose galleries stretch for one thousand kilometres: *the Scărișoara Glacier, the Cave of Bears, Bistrița Cave, the Cave of the Women, the Cave of the Bats, Ialomița Cave, the Cave of Wind, Meziad Cave.*

Romania can boast some three thousand five hundred lakes. There are volcanic lakes (*St Ana*), glacial lakes (*Bucura, Zănoaga, Gâlcescu, Bâlea*), karst lakes (Iezerul Ighiu), saline lakes (*Bottomless Lake, Ursu Lake*), natural dams (*Red Lake*), man-made reservoirs (the *Iron Gates*, on the Danube, *Izvorul Muntelui (Bicaz)*, on the Bistrița, *Vidraru*, on the Argeș, *Vidra*, on the Lotru, and *Scropoasa*, on the Ialomița).

The Lala Lake

Romania – a bit of history...

A very long time ago, during the first century A.D., the Roman legions of the Emperor Trajan made their way across the waters of the Danube into *Dacia*, the land of the "immortal" Getes (Dacians) – the ancestors of the Romanians – who worshipped the god Zalmoxis. After the Romans conquered the Dacians, part of their territory was transformed into a Roman province, named *Dacia Felix* (which is to say "Fertile Dacia"). As witness to this, there have remained the foot of the bridge over the Danube built by Apollodoros of Damascus at the orders of the Emperor Trajan, between 103 and 105 A.D., at Drobeta-Turnu Severin, and the thermal baths at Băile Herculane, as well as the ruins of forts and ancient roads. The Romans ruled for approximately 165 years in central and south-west Dacia, building roads, forts and towns (*Colonia Ulpia Traiana Sarmizegetusa, Apulum, Napoca, Potaissa, Porolissum*) and digging mines.

The Romanian nation was born of the ethnic mix of Romans and Dacians.

After the Roman withdrawal from Dacia under the Emperor Aurelian (271), the inhabitants were faced with successive waves of invaders. By the time the Hungarians arrived in the ninth century, the first autochthonous populations had already crystallised, under the leadership of the *juzi* (< Latin *judices*) and *cnezi* ("princes" < Slavic *knjazi*). The Hungarians encountered fierce resistance from the voievod states established in the Banat and Transylvania, two of the Romanian provinces. Thus, in the twelfth century, King Geza II was obliged to call on the assistance of the Germans (Saxons), to whom he accorded various privileges, in order to consolidate his power in these recently conquered regions, whose inhabitants opposed centralisation. During this period, many citadels were built, including that of Sighișoara, founded by Saxon colonists in their quality of *hospites regis* ("guests of the king"). The ruins of the peasant fortifications at Râșnov, Biertan and Cristian similarly transport us back to the atmosphere of mediaeval Transylvania.

A different Middle Ages can be discovered in the Moldavia of the famous Prince Stephen the Great, known as a tireless opponent of the Ottomans. The ruins of citadels and princely courts – such as those at Suceava, Baia, Scheia, Siret, Târgu-Neamț, Piatra-Neamț and Roman – remind us of the times when these solid and at the same time harmoniously proportioned stone edifices repelled the invading Turks.

The Romanian Land (also named Muntenia or Walachia), one of the oldest Romanian provinces, obtained its independence in 1330, after Basarab I defeated Charles Robert de Anjou at the battle of the Loviștea Depression. Many foundations – citadels, princely courts, churches, monasteries – have remained from the rulers of this "land": Neagoe Basarab (1512-1521), who built the Curtea de Argeș Monastery, Matei Basarab (1632-1654), regarded as a true "patron of the church", since he built more than thirty places of worship, Constantin Brâncoveanu (1688-1714), during whose lifetime there was a matchless flowering of culture. Hurez Monastery, the Brâncoveanu Monastery at Sâmbăta de Sus, the Church of St George the New in Bucharest, the palaces of Mogoșoaia (near Bucharest) and Potlogi (in Dâmbovița County) all bear the brilliant imprint of the Brâncoveanu style. The first capitals of Walachia were established at Câmpulung Muscel, Curtea de Argeș and Târgoviște.

After the Turks had taken control of the territory of the former Hungarian Kingdom, following the battle of Mohaci (1526), Transylvania, Moldavia and Walachia became autonomous principalities, although they were forced to recognise the suzerainity of the Ottoman Empire, to which they paid a tribute.

The Church of Curtea de Argeș Monastery

The old princely court of Wallachia at Târgoviște

In 1593, Mihai the Brave, the voievod of the Romanian Land, joined the Christian League – an anti-Ottoman coalition founded by the Pope and the Holy Roman Empire. Following the battles of Călugăreni and Giurgiu, the Romanian Land regained its independence. Mihai the Brave even succeeded in proclaiming himself "Prince of the Romanian Land, Transylvania and all Moldavia" in 1600, uniting – for the first time in history – all the Romanian territories. The union was ephemeral, however, since its initiator was killed in 1601.

Between 1716 and 1821, the Romanian Land was under the regime of the Greek Phanariots. During this period, the land was ruled by Greek princes (originally from the Phanar district of Constantinople), nominated by the Ottoman Porte. The same thing happened in Moldavia, between 1711 and 1821. The 1821 uprising led by Tudor Vladimirescu restored native rule.

Following the Austro-Turkish Peace Treaty of Karlowitz (1699), Transylvania was annexed by the Austrian Empire, under whose protectorate it remained until 1867. Between 1867 and 1918, it was part of the Austro-Hungarian Empire.

Between 1718 and 1793, Austria temporarily occupied the Romanian province of Oltenia, and the province of Bukowina between 1775 and 1918.

The former Royal Palace, Bucharest

During the Russo-Turkish War of 1828-1829, Russian troops led by Pavel Kiseleff occupied Moldova and the Romanian Land (until 1834). It might be said that the Organic Regulations (a kind of constitution) promulgated in that period were the first step towards the modern re-organisation of the Romanian principalities. They introduced for the first time the principle of the separation of executive powers and encouraged the development of new economic relations.

Between 1812 and 1918, the Moldavian province of Bassarabia was annexed by Russia.

The revolutionary ideas of 1848 also swept the Romanian provinces, although the movement was crushed at the time.

After the defeat of Russia in the Crimean War (1853-1856), the Romanian principalities came under the protection of the seven powers who signed the Paris Peace Treaty.

In 1859, Alexandru Ioan Cuza was named sole prince of Moldavia and the Romanian Land. The latter were to take the name of the United Principalities, and in 1862 became Romania, with its capital in Bucharest. Along with Mihail Kogălniceanu, Alexandru Ioan Cuza introduced a series of reforms that contributed to the modernisation of Romania.

After Cuza was deposed in 1866, Carol of Hohenzollern-Sigmaringen (Carol I) took the throne. A democratic constitution was adopted, inspired by the Belgian model.

After the Russo-Turkish War of 1877, Romania obtained complete state independence. Dobrogea, which had been ruled by the Turks since 1417, was returned to Romania.

In March 1881, Romania was proclaimed a kingdom and Carol I was named king. The long and beneficial rule of Carol I (1866-1914) was followed by the reigns of Ferdinand I (1914-1927), Mihai I (1927-1930; 1940-1947), and Carol II (1930-1940), the latter of whom imposed his own dictatorship in 1938.

At Alba Iulia, on 1 December 1918, Transylvania, the Banat, Maramureș and Crișana signed the Act of Union with Romania.

After the Second World War, Romanain territory was occupied by Soviet troops until 1958. The communists took control of the government, arresting members of the historic political parties. In 1947, King Mihai I was forced to abdicate and Romania was proclaimed a People's Republic.

The period in which Nicolae Ceaușescu was in power (1965-1989) was devastating for Romania. His dictatorship was deposed in 1989, following widespread popular anticommunist uprisings. Since 1990, democracy and a pluralist political system have been re-established and a market economy adopted.

Since 1990, Romania has established relations with the nations of the European Union, signing various accords with them. In March 2004, Romania became a mamber of NATO. In 2007, it is due to become a member of the European Union.

Alba Iulia – the place where the act of the union of the Romanian provinces was signed on 1 December 1918

Romania – UNESCO World Heritage Sites

1) The **Danube Delta** is one of the world's most extensive wetlands (2,681 square kilometres). In this exotic delta, which stretches between the fluvial branches of the Chilia, Sulina and Saint George, more than one thousand two hundred species of plants and trees, three hundred species of birds and one hundred species of fish have been identified. The Danube Delta is a veritable "Noah's Ark". Here, everything teems with life: the air hums to the wing-beat of birds (pelicans, swans, cormorants, egrets, spoonbills, widgeons, white-tailed eagles); beneath the water's surface glint fish (sturgeon, trout, perch, pike, carp); among the reeds swarm all kind of animals. In the Delta there also live turtles, snakes, vipers, otters, foxes, boar, and enots).

Almost fifty per cent of the surface area of the Danube Delta lies temporarily under water (especially in Spring), forty-five per

The Danube Delta – paradise for birds

The Danube Delta – the most extensive area of compact reed plots in the world

cent is permanently covered with water and just five per cent (sand banks) can be said to be genuinely "dry land" that never floods. Luxuriant and wild vegetation, from the beginning of the world, covers these expanses of water and earth. The Delta is in fact a labyrinth of branches, channels, swamps, lakes, sand banks and endless passages of reeds. We lose ourselves in groves of white willows or in mixed woods, formed of black poplars, trembling poplars, oaks, bushy ash, elms, and wild apple and pear trees. Here is the domain of creeping plants, such as lianas and wild vines, which inter-penetrate everywhere. The immense surfaces of rushes, bulrushes and reeds make up an unforgettable decor. The waters stretch into the distance covered in white and yellow lily pads, broken here and there by floating islands of vegetation.

The traditional fishing villages of the Danube Delta seem remnants of an ancestral world. The people from hereabouts make their living by fishing. The traditional fish dishes of these parts are highly prized. If you find yourself here, you will be able to dine on spitted fish, fish broth, pickled fish with garlic juice, and fried fishcakes. You are also sure to be tempted by a wine from the Niculițel Vineyard; the most appreciated varieties are the Aligote, the Muscat-Ottonel and the Merlot.

2) In the village of Romanii de Jos, three kilometres from Horezu (a traditional centre for pottery), you can visit the most representative complex of Romanian mediaeval architecture, definitive of the Brâncoveanu style: the **Hurez Monastery** (dating from 1690-1703). Situated in the midst of forests in the foothills of the Carpathian Mountains, the monastery comprises a main church, dedicated to the Holy Emperor Constantine and his mother St Elena (built between 1690 and 1694), the Chapel of the Birth of the Mother of God (1697), the Infirmary Church (built between 1696 and 1699 by Maria Brâncoveanu), the Hermitage of the Holy Apostles Peter and Paul (1698), the Hermitage of St Stephen (1703), the Princely House, and the Watchtower of Dionisie Bălăcescu (1752-1753).

During the time of Constantin Brâncoveanu (1688-1714), Hurez Monastery was an important centre of culture: here there was a famous scriptorium, a school for copyists, scribes and grammarians, a school for painters, where the masters who painted the murals of the foremost churches of the eighteenth century were trained, and a rich library (with four thousand volumes), unique in south-east Europe at the beginning of the eighteenth century. The museum collection at Hurez Monastery contains old church objects (books, icons, and precious fabrics), some of which date from the founding of the monastery.

The Church of Hurez Monastery

Scenes from the world of Maramureș

3) No place is more fitting than **Maramureș** in order to follow the metamorphoses of wood: this region in northern Romania is renowned for its marvellous culture of woodworking, which has flourished in the villages along the Mara, Iza, Cosău, Vișeu and Tisa valleys. The portals of the locals, which are scrupulously carved with decorative motifs representing stylised solar disks, the tree of life, crosses, geometric figures, are remarkable examples of rustic art.

Compared with massive churches of stone, the small wooden places of worship offer an alternative order of space. Expressions of local spirituality, the wooden churches in the **Maramureș villages** of Bârsana, Budești, Desești, Ieud, Plopiș, Poienile Izei, Rogoz and Șurdești, with their tapering spires soaring to the heavens, seem to have overcome the perishable nature of the material from which they have been crafted.

The **Church on the Hill at Ieud** (dedicated to the Birth of the Mother of God), dating from the seventeenth century, has murals by Alexandru Ponehalschi. In the attic were discovered the *Ieud Codices*, the oldest such codex in the Romanian language. Here there is a collection of icons from the seventeenth and eighteenth centuries, a collection of icons painted on glass from the Nicula Monastery (the first centre for painting on glass in Transylvania), precious books and documents, and carpets coloured with vegetal dyes.

The Church on the Hill (Ieud)

Church – "the house of the Lord" and "the portal to heaven"

The **Church of St Nicholas in Budești (Josani)** was erected in 1643 on the site of a church dating from the fifteenth century. The church, constructed from thick beams resting on a stone foundation, was painted in luminous, harmonious colours by Alexandru Ponehalschi in 1762. Ponehalschi was one of the most prolific mural painters in Maramureș. Unfortunately, the murals have been preserved intact only in the western part of the church. The iconostasis was also painted by Ponehalshi.

The **Church of the Blessed Parascheva in Poienile Izei** dates from the seventeenth century. The nave of the church is rectangular in plan, the porch is situated on the western side, the roof has a double hem, and the steeple, with three bells, above the porch, presents an elongated helmet, above which is fixed a tall cross. The altar differs from that of other churches in that it has four sides, as in antiquity. The murals, painted in 1794, are impressive for their eclectic style, combining traditional iconographic elements with others specific to the age.

The seventeenth century wooden **Church of the Holy Archangels Michael and Gabriel in Rogoz**, a village situated on the banks of the Lapuș, was constructed in 1633. This place of worship is one of the most interesting in all of Maramureș. The nave is rectangular, the narthex has apses, while the altar is hexagonal. The belfry is flanked by four turrets, placed at each corner. Beneath the eaves can be found numerous consoles, sculpted in the form of horses' heads.

The **Church of the Blessed Parascheva in Desești** was erected in 1717 (or in 1770, according to others). Its architecture is in the traditional style: the joinery, the equilibrium of forms and volumes, the harmony of the whole confer an impression of simplicity and elegance. Originality is lent to the monument by the beams of the upper part, supporting the sloping roof, which are elongated and sculpted into steps.

Children learning Maramureș folk dances

The wooden church at Plopiș

The **Church of St Nicholas** (eighteenth century) **in Bârsana** offers us a typical example of Maramureș architecture. The church is remarkable for its small scale, rectangular plan, five-sided apse, belfry situated over the porch, and the double slope of the roof. The murals were painted in 1806 by two local artists, and the composition was influenced by baroque art.

The **Church of the Holy Archangels Michael and Gabriel in Plopiș** was built at the end of the eighteenth century by Ioan Macarie and the murals were painted in 1811 by Ștefan of Șișești. The originality of this church lies in the three-lobed ceiling vault of the nave, a case unique in the wooden churches of Maramureș.

The **Church of the Holy Archangels Michael and Gabriel in Șurdești**, a village in the Cavnic River valley, was built in 1766 and the murals were painted in 1783 by Ștefan of Șișești. It is thought to be the tallest religious wooden edifice in Europe, with a tower of fifty-four metres. The porch has two rows of arcades, one above the other. The iconostasis of the church is remarkable for its polychrome, gilded baroque wooden ornamentation, a true treasure of old Romanian art.

Travellers are recommended not to miss these monuments representative of the wooden architecture of Maramureș, veritable treasures of old Romanian art.

Sighișoara citadel

4) Sighișoara, one of the few inhabited citadels in the world, is a beautiful illustration of mediaeval city building. The Sighișoara citadel, built in 1191 by Saxon colonists on a hill overlooking the left bank of the Târnava Mare River, has preserved precisely the elements of the mediaeval universe. After we enter this miraculous space, passing beneath the arcade of the old Clock Tower, which for centuries has measured the tireless flow of time, we arrive in the central square of the citadel. It was here that, in days gone by, trials were held and executions carried out. It was also here that the "pole of infamy" was to be found, to which evildoers were bound, with a six kilogram stone hanging from their neck. Then we enter the church of the former Dominican monastery, founded in the thirteenth century, with its baroque altar, sculpted in 1680 by Johann West and painted by wandering artist Jeremias Stranovius. Hence we pass by the Venetian House, the House of Vlad Dracul and the Stag House, before venturing down one of the narrow cobbled streets that wind down the hill, lined with old houses painted in pastel shades and with wooden shutters. We pass beneath street lamps that cast their ghostly light in the shadows of evening, we climb the one hundred and seventy-five steps of the Scholars' Stair before reaching the highest point of the citadel, where can be found the fourteenth century Church on the Hill, an impressive monument of Gothic architecture. Hence we descend by the old fourteenth century walls, which, at a length of 920 m enclose the

Citadel Hill, formerly bolstered by redoubtable bastions and fourteen defence turrets, of which nine have been preserved. The citadel was once inhabited mainly by craftsmen, who – as is known – dominated material production in the Middle Ages. They occupied a central place in the life of the community, and were responsible for the material support of the church and the citadel's defensive system. As such, the richest guilds each had to defend and maintain a tower and a section of the defensive wall. The towers thus came to be named after the guilds that tended them: in Sighișoara we can see the Towers of the Tanners, Tinsmiths, Ropers, Butchers, Furriers, Tailors, Cobblers and Blacksmiths.

Walking through the old citadel of Sighișoara, with its approximately one hundred and fifty inhabited buildings, most of which are more than three hundred years old, we may, with a little imagination, reconstruct a number of aspects of everyday mediaeval life. In any case, every year, for three days in the last week of July, Sighișoara returns to the Middle Ages: knights in shining armour compete in tournaments, there are witch trials, ladies in resplendent gowns appear everywhere, minstrels sing their songs, and on every street corner there are improvised plays, concerts of mediaeval music and all kinds of other performances... During the *Festival of Mediaeval Arts*, the streets of the citadel are thronged with the thousands of tourists who come to take part in this picturesque event.

The Clock Tower and the Stag House, Sighișoara

5) Nowhere in Romania can more churches, monasteries, and hermitages be found in such a compact area as in **Moldavia.** Believe it or not, most of them are hundreds of years old.

Built especially by the Moldavian voievodes of the Mușatin family (Petru Mușat I, Iliaș, Petru, Alexandru the Good, Bogdan II, Stephen the Great, Petru Rareș), these splendid monasteries at the same time served as the princely necropolis. According to the chronicler Ion Neculce, Stephen the Great (1457-1504), "the bastion of Christianity", during his forty-seven year reign, built a church or a monastery after each of his battles against the Turks, Hungarians or Poles. It is not known how much truth there is in this statement, but it is certain that the prince left dozens of places of worship. The Reign of Petru Rareș (1527-1538; 1541-1546) continued the tradition of the great voievod Stephen. From this period date the priceless murals at Arbore, Voroneț, Humor, Moldovița, and Probota, churches all listed by UNESCO as world heritage sites.

The exterior walls of a number of churches in Moldavia are covered in murals painted in incomparable hues of red, yellow, blue and green. Those who see them will never forget these ancient images of the sacred and profane history of the world.

Exterior murals

The Church of Voroneț Monastery

The **Monastery of Voroneț**, five kilometres from Gura Humorului, is considered the "Sistine Chapel of the East". On the west facade of the church founded by Stephen the Great in 1488, there is a depiction of the Last Judgement. It was painted between 1534 and 1535 against a background whose inimitable shade of blue has long become famous... The origin of the "Voroneț blue" have still not been elucidated.

The **Church of the Beheading of John the Baptist** (1503) in the village of **Arbore**, thirty-two kilometres north-west of Suceava, was part of the boyar court of Luca Arbore, the gatekeeper of Suceava in the time of Stephen the Great. The exterior murals were painted in 1541 by Dragoș Coman of Iași, reckoned "a true Pisanello of Moldavia, the greatest artist of the Orthodox East in the sixteenth century". In the porch can be found the tomb of the founder, the most representative gothic funerary monument in all Moldavia.

The **church of the Humor Monastery**, situated six kilometres north of the town of Gura Humorului, is one of the most impressive monuments of Romanian mediaeval art. It was built in the year 1530 by Tudor Bubuiog the Logothete, the commander of Petru Rareș' artillery. It preserves the admirable Byzantine murals painted in 1535 by Toma Zugravul of Suceava. The predominant colour is brick red, which distinguishes it chromatically from other such churches.

Moldovița, founded in 1532 by Petru Rareș, is one of the most beautiful of all the churches with exterior murals in Bukowina. It is remarkable for the golden lustre of its murals, executed by Toma of Suceava in 1537. The best known of the mural scenes is the *Siege of Constantinople*, on the south facade.

Sucevița Monastery

Under the sign of the sacral

The **Monastery of Sucevița**, the most fortified of the monastic complexes of Moldavia, dates from 1581-1601. It is situated eighteen kilometres west of Rădăuți. The exterior murals of this Movilești foundation are remarkable for their chromatic refinement, painted against a predominantly green background. Most impressive is the scene representing the ladder of the virtues, painted on the north face. It is regarded as the last representative example of the architectural style that crystallised in the epoch of Stephen the Great.

The **Probota Monastery**, situated five kilometres from the town of Dolhasca, was built in 1530 by Petru Rareș. It is one of the greatest achievements of Moldavian feudal architecture of the sixteenth century. The monastery church has both interior and exterior murals, painted in 1532 in the style of the Rareș epoch. The murals were recently restored.

The world of the Transylvanian Saxons

The Church at Pătrăuți, twelve kilometres from Suceava, was founded by Stephen the Great in 1487.

Construction of the **Church of St George at the Monastery of St John the New in Suceava** was begun during the time of Bogdan III (1514), the son of Stephen the Great, and was completed by Ștefaniță Vodă in 1522. Of the exterior murals, dating from the time of Petru Rareș (1532-1534), only fragments have been preserved, on the south wall. The church houses the relics of St John the New, brought to Suceava in 1402 by Alexandru the Good and initially housed in Mirăuți Church. Since 1991, the Monastery of St John the New has been the see of the Archbishopric of Suceava and Rădăuți.

6) At the centre of the rural settlements founded by Saxon colonists in the Romanian province of Transylvania in the twelfth century stood a fortified church, which also served as a place of refuge in case of danger. The **fortified churches of Transylvania**, which look like small citadels, were built in particular after the Tartar invasion of 1241. There are approximately one hundred and fifty villages which preserve such monuments. Seven of these churches have been named UNESCO world heritage sites.

Within the peasant citadel in the village of **Biertan** (Sibiu County), a fortified church in the late gothic style was constructed between 1492 and 1516. The fortified complex consists of three precincts, protected by towers and bastions. The open-plan church preserves a polyptic altar with fifteenth-century polychrome wood carvings, choir stalls carved in the Renaissance style by master craftsman Johannes Reymucht of Sighișoara in 1514, and a stone pulpit, decorated with carvings inspired by the *Passion* cycle, attributed to mason Ulrich of Brașov (1523). From 1572, the church was, for almost three centuries, the Episcopal See of the Evangelical Church.

In the village of **Câlnic** (Alba County) can be found one of the oldest citadels in Transylvania, erected around 1200. Within the oval-shaped precincts, there are a chapel, the three-storey Siegfried Tower and two watchtowers.

In the village of **Dârjiu** (Harghita County), attested in documents in 1334, a Romanesque-style church was constructed in the thirteenth and fourteenth centuries. It was subsequently transformed in the gothic style and then fortified. The interior preserves gothic-style murals executed in 1419. Remarkable are the scenes illustrating the *legend of Ladislas* (inspired by the war waged by the Ladislas the Holy against the Cumanians in the eleventh century) and the *Conversion of St Paul.*

Fortified churches of Transylvania

The Gothic Church at Viscri

The fortified church at **Prejmer** (Brașov County), a foundation attested in 1240, was built between 1241 and 1250 in the early gothic style with Cistercian influences. It preserves a priceless polyptic altar, painted in the fifteenth century, and an organ dating from 1803. The Prejmer fortification, dating from the fifteenth to sixteenth centuries, is the strongest peasant citadel in Transylvania. The walls are six metres thick and fourteen metres high.

The church at the centre of the village of **Saschiz** (Mureș County) was built between 1493 and 1496. It has a single nave, an elongated choir and polygonal apses.

The settlement of **Valea Viilor** (Sibiu County), formerly named Vorumloc, preserves a beautiful fortified church, dedicated to St Peter. It was built in the thirteenth century; at the end of the fifteenth century, it was surrounded by eight metre-high, strong defensive walls, equipped with turrets. It preserves a gothic tabernacle and choir stalls in the early Renaissance style (1518).

In the middle of the peasant fortress at **Viscri** (Brașov County), erected in the fifteenth century, there is a gothic church, constructed on the site of a Romanesque chapel from the twelfth to thirteenth centuries.

7) The nucleus of the Dacian kingdom was to be found in the **Orăștiei Mountains** in the south-west of Transylvania. The **Dacian fortresses**, built in the first century BC and the first century AD, which are preserved at the edge of these mountains are among the few vestiges of these legendary ancestors of the Romanians, who considered themselves "immortals". These fortresses, enclosed by perfectly fitting walls of polished limestone blocks (*murus dacicus*), represent a "defensive system unique in European architecture". Countless forts, strategic constructions and watchtowers cover a 200 square kilometre area of the Orăștiei Mountains. The numerous sanctuaries discovered in their vicinity are a testament to the profoundly religious spirit of this mysterious people, about whom few things are known with certainty. The original combination of religious and military architectural elements characterises these citadels from the classical phase of Dacian civilisation.

Dacian vestiges

The sanctuary of the Dacian settlement at Sarmizegetusa Regia

The military, political, economic and religious centre of the Dacians was **Sarmizegetusa Regia** (now the village of Grădiștea de Munte, in the commune of Orăștioara, Hunedoara County). It is situated 1,200 metres above sea level, at the highest point of Grădiștea Hill. Many manmade terraces were carved out of the hillside. The upper plateau is connected to the sacred area of the sanctuaries on two terraces by a sacred way – a monumental paved road with limestone flags. Before it was conquered and destroyed by the Romans, Sarmizegetusa Regia was the most important metallurgical centre anywhere in Europe outside the Roman Empire.

Al the access routes to this capital were protected by numerous other strategically placed citadels. These include:

- **Costești-Cetățuie** (commune of Orăștioara, Hunedoara County), built by master craftsmen and architects brought from the Greek Black Sea colonies
- **Costești -Blidaru** (commune of Orăștioara, Hunedoara County)
- **Luncani-Piatra Roșie** (commune of Boșorod, Hunedoara County)
- **Bănița** (Hunedoara County)
- **Căpâlna** (commune of Săsciori, Alba County)

Romanian itineraries

1) The Black Sea

The length of the southern Romanian coast, which stretches from Cape Midia to Vama Veche, we can find both wild rocky shorelines and exotic beaches of fine sand.

In Antiquity, it used to be called the *Pontus Euxinus*, or the "Hospitable Sea". Today, the Black Sea – or rather its coast – is besieged every summer by tourists, who come here to enjoy the sun and seawater. There are numerous resorts for tourists: *Mamaia, Năvodari, Eforie Nord, Eforie Sud, Olimp, Costinești, Neptun, Jupiter, Venus, Saturn, Mangalia.*

In May 2006, the *Foundation for Environmental Education* (FEE) accorded, for the first time in Romania, Blue Flag status to seven beaches: the Lido at Mamaia, Adras at Saturn, Cristi's Comimpex and Sun Paradise at Olimp, Europa and Giovani at Eforie Nord, Perla Venusului at Venus, and for the tourist harbour at Eforie Nord.

The Casino at Constanța

Mamaia (three kilometres north of Constanța), situated on a coastal strip between the Black Sea and Lake Siutghiol, offers elegant three, four and five star hotels, open-air swimming pools, sports fields, amusement parks, discotheques, an open-air theatre, a dolphinarium and a planetarium. In the holiday village, you will find restaurants decorated in the styles typical of the different regions of Romania.

Eforie Nord (fourteen kilometres south of Constanța) developed after 1894, when Eforia Spitalelor Civile of Bucharest constructed a sanatorium here. The two treatment centres have hot bath installations (with concentrated salt water from Lake Techirghiol and from the sea).

Eforie Sud (eighteen kilometres south of Constanța) is remarkable for its wonderful maritime riviera, which descends in successive stages to a beach two kilometres long. From the cliffs, there is a wonderful view. Until 1950, it was named *Carmen Sylva* (the pen name of Queen Elisabeta, the wife of King Carol I). It was here that the first balneary establishment in Dobrogea was founded in 1892.

On holiday, in the Romanian coastal resorts

Don't miss taking a boat trip on the open sea

Costinești (twenty-eight kilometres south of Constanța) is a favourite resort for young people in Romania. The Costinești beach, oriented towards the south, is exposed to the sun all day, a privilege which can be boasted by very few European beaches. The beach is equipped for thalassotherapy and heliotherapy.

Mangalia (forty-four kilometres from Constanța), the southernmost resort on the Romanian coast, developed on the site of the ancient colony of *Callatis*, founded by the Greeks in the sixth century BC, and was revitalised by the Genoese (in the thirteenth and fourteenth centuries), who named it *Pangalia*. It is the only coastal resort in which mineral springs can be found (sulphurous, mezothermal and radioactive). Three kilometres from the municipality of Mangalia can be found Herghelia Mangalia, with its hippodrome. In Mangalia, we can see the vestiges of a Roman-Byzantine basillicum dating from the fifth century, the mosque of Esmahan Sultan (1590), in the Moorish style, and the Museum of Archaeology.

Venus (three kilometres north of Mangalia) is situated on a sloping promontory, which forms a natural amphitheatre. We may remark here the variety of architectural styles displayed by the hotels, which mostly have female names (*Anca, Corina, Dana, Felicia, Irina, Raluca, Rodica, Silvia*). At the south of the resort, there is a pavilion for mud and sulphur baths.

Jupiter (five kilometres north of Mangalia) is a summer resort situated between the Comorova Woods and the seashore. The beach at Jupiter, which stretches for one kilometre along the gulf, is especially picturesque.

The climate of the Romanian Black Sea coast is temperate continental, with light marine influences. In summer, the average temperature is 22 degrees Celsius. Romanian beaches have the advantage of being exposed to the sun for between ten and twelve hours a day. On torrid days (when the surface temperature of the beach rises to forty degrees Celsius), the marine breezes, rich in aerosols, cool the atmosphere. Given its quite reduced salinity, the Black Sea offers optimal conditions for sub-aquatic and nautical sports. Swimming enthusiasts have nothing to fear here from currents or dangerous marine animals. At Mangalia or Neptun, there are opportunities to take special thalassotherapy cures, or treatment with Gerovital and Aslavital, famous Romanian products which prevent premature ageing and reinvigorate the body. The organogenous mud of Lake Techirgiol has curative properties renowned throughout the world.

The Black Sea Coast

The *Tropaeum Traiani* triumphal monument at Adamclisi

Dobrogea, situated in south-east Romania, between the Danube and the Black Sea, is one of the most picturesque regions of Romania. Formerly inhabited by Getes and Scythians, the region was colonised by the Greeks in the seventh and sixth centuries BC, then became part of the state formed by Burebista, was absorbed by the Roman and Byzantine Empire, and then by the Romanian Land, in the time of Mircea the Old. Over the settlements of Dobrogea there still floats the perfume of the Levant, reminding us of the times when these places were under Turkish rule (1417-1878). After the Russo-Turkish War of 1877-1878, Dobrogea once more became part of a Romanian state.

In the commune of *Adamclisi* are preserved the ruins of the *Tropaeum Traiani* citadel and the triumphal monument erected by the Emperor Trajan to honour his victory over the Dacians.

2) The Prahova Valley

The Prahova Valley is one of the most popular regions of Romania for tourists.

The Prahova River springs from beneath the Predeal Pass, at an altitude of 1,020 metres. The Prahova flows between the Bucegi Mountains on the right and the Baiului Mountains on the left as far as Posada. This is the upper (or montane) section of the Prahova Valley, with a length of thirty-three kilometres. Over a stretch of just 25 kilometres, there is a chain of attractive tourist resorts (*Predeal, Azuga, Buşteni, Poiana Ţapului, Sinaia*), which are the perfect base for unforgettable walks in the mountains by which they are flanked. These resorts began to develop after King Carol I established his summer residence in Sinaia, in 1866, and after an international railway line was laid through the region.

Predeal is situated on the crest that separates the Prahova Valley from the Timiş Valley, twenty-five kilometres south of Braşov and 147 km north of Bucharest on the (DN1/E60 road). It is flanked by the peaks of Piatra Mare, Postăvaru and Clăbucet. Predeal began to develop as a resort after 1918. It is the highest altitude settlement in Romania (1,020-1,160 m) and is endowed with nine ski slopes, which total about ten kilometres and are served by two ski lifts and three cable cars. Predeal is the ideal place for winter sports; there is snow cover, with a depth that can reach a few metres, for more than one hundred days per year. Hikers can choose between the numerous routes to the mountain chalets in the area: Trei Brazi, Clăbucet-Sosire, Clăbucet-Plecare, Gârbova, Susai, Piatra Mare, Poiana Secuilor, Timiş, Cerbul.

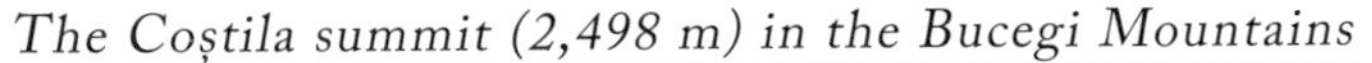

The Coştila summit (2,498 m) in the Bucegi Mountains

Unusual limestone relief

Situated in the foothills of the Bucegi Mountains, at an altitude of 895-950 metres, *Azuga* is 135 km from Bucharest and 36 km from Brașov. It is known as "skiers' paradise". The Azuga winter sports complex includes: the Cazacu slope (with a length of 3,050 metres and a difference in level of 758 metres), the only slope confirmed by the FIS in Romania, equipped with a cable car and snow maintenance machines; the Sorica slope (2,100 metres long, with a gradient of 29 in one thousand); eighteen kilometres of slopes for on and off piste skiing; a slope for snowboarding; and ski lifts.

Bușteni, situated in the foothills of the Caraiman Massif and Baiului Mountains, at an altitude of 880-940 metres, stretches for seven kilometres, between Vadul Cerbului and the tunnel bored through the Muchia Lungă Mountain. Above Bușteni loom the steep rocky walls of the Bucegi Mountains, which mountaineers can explore on the 250 difficulty-graded routes. Here one can believe in the "Alps of the East".

Bușteni is known as the "Gateway to the Bucegi Mountains". Before our eyes rear the dizzying heights of the Bucegi Massif, which was declared a national park in 1990 and has a total of 35,700 hectares. On top of this mountain, at an altitude of 1,800 to 2,000 metres, has developed an erosion platform (the Bucegi Plateau), stretching for about ten kilometres and covered with alpine meadows. As a result of climactic factors (wind, freezing/thawing), strange, megalithic forms have developed – *the Old Women, the Sphinx, the Mushrooms, Hermes, Zalmoxis*. In 1978, the area became linked to the Bucegi Mountain Plateau by a cable car. The Bușteni-Babele cable car, covering a distance of 4,350 metres, is the longest in Romania and the third longest in Europe. The *Babele chalet* is linked to the *Peștera Hotel*, next to the Ialomița Cave, by a cable car covering a distance of 2,611 metres. The Kalinderu ski slope (with a length of 1,500 metres), sited on a slope of the Caraiman Masif, one kilometre from the centre of Bușteni, is equipped with lighting, a tele-gondola, and a snow-making machine.

On the Șaua Mare platform of Caraiman, at an altitude of 2,291 metres, towers the imposing *Cross of Heroes*, with a height of thirty-three metres. It was constructed between 1926 and 1928, at the initiative of Queen Maria, in memory of the soldiers who fell during fighting in the Prahova Valley, in the First World War. The Cross, the most valuable historic mountain monument in Romania, is unique in Europe and was fabricated from metal struts, welded into a harmonious network. It is mounted on a seven and a half metre-high plinth, made of reinforced concrete plated in stone, in the form of a truncated pyramid, inside which is mounted an electric generator that powers one hundred and twenty 500 Watt bulbs fixed around the outline of the cross.

At No. 1 Zamora Street can be found the *Cantacuzino Castle*, built in 1910 by Prince Gheorghe Grigore Cantacuzino, known as the "Nabab", who was also a minister.

The Cross of Heroes on Mount Caraiman

Castle Peleș, Sinaia

The bijou resort of *Sinaia*, considered the "Pearl of the Carpathians", situated in the foothills of the Bucegi Mountains, flanked by the Vârful cu Dor peak, and by the Furnica and Piatra Arsă peaks, is 122 km from Bucharest and 49 km from Brașov. The hamlet grew up around the Sinaia Monastery, founded in 1690-1695 by Sword-bearer Mihail Cantacuzino, after the model of the *St Elena Monastery* on Mount Sinai.

Carol I of Hohenzollern-Sigmarigen, the first King of Romania, charmed by the setting of Sinaia, decided in 1866 to establish his summer residence here. *Peleș Castle* was built between 1875 and 1883, and bore the imprint of the German neo-Renaissance style. The plans were drawn up by architects Wilhelm von Doderer and Johann Schulz from Lemberg. Between 1896 and 1914, architects

Karel Liman and André Lecomte de Noüy worked on extending and stylistically redefining the castle, superimposing upon it a neo-gothic style. After 1953, Peleș Castle was turned into a museum. In the museum's collection there are paintings and engravings (Rembrandt, El Greco, Raphael, Correggio, Murillo, Velasquez, Bruegel), sculptures, armour, medals, oriental carpets, pieces of furniture, period costumes, Flemish and French tapestries, Swiss and German stained glass from the fifteenth to eighteenth centuries, rare books, Japanese ceramics, English silverware etc. The nearby Pelișor Castle was the residence of the royal couple Ferdinand and Maria.

At the *Luminiș Villa* in the Cumpătu district, which belonged to composer George Enescu, there is a memorial museum, financed by the Sinaia European Cultural Centre.

In Sinaia, winter sports enthusiasts will find alpine ski slopes, on and off-piste skiing, with varying degrees of difficulty and sledge slopes.

On the D1 (E60) between Comarnic and Câmpina can be fond Breaza, one of the best-rated resorts in Romania. It is said that this town, situated in the Prahova Sub-Carpathians, has the most sunny days in the country. Breaza air, loaded with ozone and negative ions, has been compared to that of the Davos resort in the Swiss Alps. The first private golf club in Romania was established at Breaza: *Lac de Verde.*

Golf course at Breaza

Maramureș – a world of the picturesque

3) Maramureș

Maramureș is, as the old ballad goes, "*a land old and fair, whose people are beyond compare*". The villages are unique in Romania. Every year they are invaded by tourists in search of the archaic and picturesque atmosphere of times gone by. All of them want to see the magnificent wooden portals and churches, to take part in the celebration of old customs, to drink *horinca* and eat bacon three fingers thick, to admire the traditional costume of the villagers, to ride the archaic steam train along the Vaser Valley, to visit the Merry Cemetery at Săpânța...

Rural traditions at Mara

The villages nestling in the Mara, Iza, Cosău and Tisa valleys are included in all the tourist itineraries through Maramureș. In no other region of Romania is agricultural tourism as well developed as here. Why are the villages of Maramureș so sought after by the tourists? Perhaps it is because of the atypical image they offer: although they manage to remain in touch with today's world, they have not renounced the ways handed down by their forefathers. Each village offers us the image of a complete world, with well-established values, passed down from generation to generation. "Authentic" is the adjective that best characterises these villages. Old technologies (such as the *vâltoare*, a primitive hydraulic device, by means of which the peasants wash their clothes, or the *horincie*, an installation used in the preparation of the local beverage), houses built in the traditional style, and pastoral customs stand as witness to a universe unspoilt by time. At the centre of each community, there is a wooden church with tall steeple, adorned with handcrafted carvings (see the chapter on UNESCO heritage sites in Romania). Around the church, on Sundays and religious holidays, revolves the entire soul of the village. On such occasions, you will have the chance to see a veritable parade of Maramureș traditional costumes.

4) Bucowina

The exterior murals of the churches of Bucowina (see the chapter on UNESCO world heritage sites in Romania) are, of course, the objective of all those who travel through this ancient Moldavian province. The charm of Bucowina, however, also resides in its rolling hills (parallel chains of summits cloaked in forests of fir, beech or spruce), the winding Bistrița and Moldovița rivers, the steep Călimani Mountains, with the *Twelve Apostles* Rocks, and the beautiful local customs.

If you have arrived in Bucowina and you have not stopped off in its villages enveloped in a picturesque archaic atmosphere, which is paradoxically not at all anachronistic, since everything pulsates with life, then you have not yet seen anything. If you have arrived in Bucowina and you have not talked at length with its inhabitants, for whom respect for tradition is a natural fact, then you have not yet discovered its charm. You will be able to feast your ears on the ballads, *doinas* (traditional songs) and carols, and your eyes on the colourful peasant rugs, which are woven on the loom at home and used as carpets or to decorate the walls. Only then will you be able to understand the

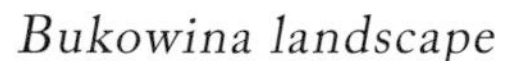
Bukowina landscape

In Bukowina, tradition takes precedence

depths of the folk spirit. You would also do well to visit the potters' workshops at Marginea and Rădăuți, which religiously preserve the secrets of ancient techniques for making polished black ceramic vases, or vases decorated with rich floral motifs. Then you should seek out the astonishing transformations of wood. Here in Bucowina, where a veritable civilisation of woodcarving has flourished, the beautiful houses with open porches and churches with meticulous carving are like jewels. The horns for gunpowder, the women's blouses, the cloths from Humor Monastery, the singlets from Vama garnished with marten fur, the long peasant coats from Straja, pyro-engraved water jugs, the barrels for storing beverages, the New Year masks, the painted eggs – all seem like exhibits from an ethnographic museum. But this is merely an impression, for if you look closely you will find that they are not at all lifeless objects, but rather they make up part of the everyday life of the people of Bucowina.

5) The Rucăr-Bran corridor

Between Bran and Rucăr, for a distance of just twenty-two kilometres, stretches a fairytale area of rustic settlements dotted along a low-lying corridor flanked on the one side by the Piatra Craiului Mountains, and on the other by the Bucegi Mountains. Hundreds of years ago, this was a trade route, linking Brașov and Câmpulung. Nowadays, it is an area of knolls, crevasses and hills still traversed by the flocks of shepherds who know the ancient techniques of making cheese in fir bark, an area that has become a favourite destination for tourists. Traversing the villages between Bran and Rucăr, we can be convinced that rural, ecological and cultural tourism can be fully functional in Romania.

Bran is known as an ancient pastoral settlement, in which the phenomenon of transhumation can still be witnessed. Each year, on the last Saturday of September, the *festival of the scattering of the sheep* takes place (the sheep are brought down from the mountains and returned to their owners), on which occasion the best rearer of animals is named. You can also take part in the following festivals: the *Pantelimon Fair*, on 9 August; *the festival of the first milking of the sheep*, in September; *the Fair of the Holy Archangels Michael and Gabriel*, on 8 November; *the Days of Bran*, in August. If you wish to familiarise yourself with the traditions of Bran folk, then you can participate in the one day "At Home with Traditional Craftsmen" tours. You will learn the secrets of the furrier, of hand weaving, knitting, embroidery, and joinery; you will learn the way eggs are painted at Bran, how to weave wicker baskets, to make masks and dolls, to paint icons on glass and wood.

View towards the crest of Piatra Craiului

In the winter of 2004-2005, a small but modern ski slope was opened in Bran, equipped with chair lifts. The Zănoaga slope (length: 800 metres) is situated in the Poarta Valley, about four kilometres from Bran. In order to get there, you will have to forget about your car, but you will take one of the horse-drawn sleighs that go from the centre of Bran or from in front of the guesthouses.

Walk through the villages of the Bran commune – *Poarta, Predeluț, Șimon, Sohodol* – and admire the proud, Transylvanian-style houses scattered amid the hills and valleys. The centres of these settlements are dominated by old churches, built by shepherds in the eighteenth century.

Hiking enthusiasts will not be disappointed; from the village of Poarta, there are three marked trails that lead to the Omu Peak (Bucegi Mountains). In the village of Șimon, there is also access to the Bucegi Mountains. From Bran you can set off towards *Zărnești*, the gateway to the Piatra Craiului Mountains, twenty kilometres away. Piatra Craiului, the most spectacular massif in the Romanian Carpathians, regarded as a "morphologic accident", is an isolated limestone crest, which stretches from Zărnești to Podu Dâmboviței for a length of twenty-five kilometres. In this massif, consisting of limestone dating from the Jurassic Age, there are numerous karst formations. The massif is renowned for its approximately 160 caves (*Dâmbovicioara, the Cave of Bears, the Cave of Devils, Stanciu*) and its twenty-three gorges (*Dâmboviței, Dâmbovicioara, Brusturet*).

The Dâmbovicioara Cave

The Rucăr-Bran corridor

Everyone wants to see Bran first and foremost... It is no less true, however, that after Bran comes a chain of discreet little villages, with less resonant names, whose atmosphere makes any stay delightful. The villages of *Cheia, Măgura, Drumul Carului, Peștera, Fundata, Fundățica, Șirnea, Ciocanul, Podu Dâmboviței, and Dâmbovicioara* can all compete with the most renowned mountain resorts. The specific local character has been preserved intact, in spite of the tourist boom – something which is exceptional in our day and age! And it would be a pity if it did not remain thus. The villagers here have the wise knowledge of how to balance two different things: even if they have opened their doors to tourists, accepting the laws of the agricultural tourism market, they have not neglected their own business – they continue to take their sheep to pasture, make their delicious cheeses and work the wool. Every year, at the end of August, at Fundata – an ancient pastoral settlement – the festival of *Nedeia* is celebrated. Nedeia is a wonderful occasion for all the inhabitants of the villages around Bran, as they gather to converse, to listen to traditional music, to dance the *hora*, to admire the traditional costumes and to sell their wares.

6) Castle Bran

Whoever comes to Bran should without fail visit Castle Bran, built in 1212 by a Teuton knight. Today, Castle Bran has become synonymous with Vlad the Impaler, alias Dracula. Whether we like it or not, however, the history of the castle has very little links to the character in question.

Previously, King Andrei II of Hungary (1176-1235) had set up the Order of Teuton Knights in the Bârsa Land, recently conquered by the Hungarians. The knights were given the task of defending the eastern border of the land against the Cumanians and of spreading Catholicism among the "pagans". Fourteen years later, in 1225, the Teutons were driven out, following armed conflict. In the meantime, they had built around seven castles, including Bran. In 1212, one of these German knights, Dietrich or Theoderic by name, had constructed a wooden fortress on top of a sixty-metre high

Castle Bran – former residence of Queen Maria

crag, which then came to be known as the *Dietrichstein* or *Lapis Tyderici*. It is seems that the German name *Törzburg* derives hence, becoming *Torcs* or *Terch* in Hungarian. The latter is the origin of the Romanian name Turciu, as the citadel was to be called until 1474. It is only after this date that the castle, now a defensive bastion against Ottoman invasion, was to be known as Bran, from the Slavonic *Brana* ("gate"). The old name of the citadel is now recalled only by the River Turcul, which flows nearby.

In 1377, the Saxons of the Bârsa Land, who had conquered the Teutons' fortifications at the end of the thirteenth century, built a stone castle in its place. These events took place during the reign of Hungarian King Ludovic I of Anjou (1342-1382), who had accorded the Saxons the right to build "at their own expense and effort". In 1369, there occurred the first Turkish incursion into Wallachia. As a result, in March 1395, Mircea the Old (1386-1418) forged an alliance with the King of Hungary, Sigismund of Luxemburg (1386-1437): the two monarchs promised to support each other in the struggle against the Ottoman armies. On the occasion of the treaty, Sigismund gave Mircea two castles, one of them at Bran. In 1419, Sigismund took back the castle from Mihail, Mircea's son and successor, and entrusted it to the Szekler county, subordinate to the voievod of Transylvania. Later, Iancu of Hunedoara (1441-1456) repaired and strengthened Bran, then entrusted the defence of southern Transylvania to Vlad the Impaler, who had lost the throne of Wallachia. It is highly possible that the Impaler may have visited Bran, which was an important border post, but there is no historical evidence to this effect. Bran was later to enter into the hands of the citizens of Brașov, from whom it was fraudulently seized by the Voievod of Transylvania, Gabriel Bathory (1608-1613), in 1612. Prince Gabriel Bethlen (1613-1629) renovated the castle in the Renaissance style. In 1651, Prince Rakoczy II (1648-1660) sold the castle back to the people of Brașov, who were to own it until the twentieth century.

Although the castle was solely military in scope, in time it came to have a mainly commercial role, as the customs point between Transylvania and Muntenia. After the customs point was moved from Bran to Giuvala, the castle lost its economic importance.

On 1 December 1920, the Town Council of Brașov donated Castle Bran to Queen Maria, in recognition of her contribution to the achievement of the Great Union of 1 December 1918.

Castle Bran, built in the 13th Century by Teutonic knights

From the moment Castle Bran entered into her possession, Queen Maria began thinking of the changes that had to be made in order to transform it into her summer residence. Between 1920 and 1927, the court architect, Karel Liman, supervised the restoration work. The military aspect of the castle was "softened". It is true that the exterior could not be modified very much, but on the other hand the interiors were subject to astonishing changes: the Great Hall, decorated in the German Renaissance style; the Yellow Room, the Music Room, King Carol the Second's Tyrolean Chamber, Prince Nicolae's Saxon Chamber etc.) Furniture was brought from Venice, Florence, Spain and Germany. A number of rooms were furnished in the old Romanian and Saxon styles. Various accessories "lightened" the atmosphere of the sombre walls of former days: precious vases, Russian ceramics, Turkish and English chandeliers, old icons, paintings, Baroque statuettes. A third and fourth floor were added to the building, as well as two towers for staircases. Two loggias were built: one in the inner courtyard, the other on the third floor. A chapel, with murals painted by Arthur Verona in 1927, was installed on the ground floor of one of the towers and a terrace on the fourth floor. The stoves were transformed into fireplaces and the merlons into windows.

Tourists may now visit a castle that combines both Gothic and Renaissance elements with rustic Transylvanian architecture. The castle houses the Bran Museum, where the public can view priceless collections of mediaeval art and artefacts: furniture, painting, sculpture, and icons on wood and on glass.

In 1987, a Customs Museum was inaugurated in the old mediaeval customs house at Bran. It is known that through these parts passed goods on their way to Flanders, Germany, Turkey, the Middle East etc. On display there are documents regarding the type of goods in transit through the Bran Pass, as well as maps, mediaeval coins, seals, weighing instruments, and vehicles.

In the castle park there is a Museum of Bran Village, where one can see various types of peasant household and traditional installations (for the working of wood or wool, for example).

Interior courtyard of Bran Castle

7) The Danube Cauldrons

The Danube offers us an overwhelming spectacle along the length of its wild gorge, forming the south-western border of Romania between Baziaș and Drobeta-Turnu Severin! However, the Cauldrons stretch is yet more breathtaking still: for nine kilometres, the Danube snakes between the mountain walls of Ciucaru Mic (310 m) and Ciucaru Mare (318), on the Romanian bank, and Mali Strbac (626 m) and Veliki Strbac (768 m) on the Serbian side. The width of the Greater and Lesser Cauldrons, which wind through the Dubova Basin, does not exceed 150-350 metres. In the past, the waters were thought to "boil" and seethe here, as if in a fisherman's cauldron. It was thus that the area came to be known as the Cauldrons.

The construction of the Iron Gates I hydroelectric dam at Gura Văii between 1964 and 1971 raised the water level by 33 metres, solving the problem of Danube navigation, which had, until then, been complicated and fraught with danger, due to rocks, shelves, whirlpools and all kinds of natural obstacles.

The are around the Danube Cauldrons has been declared a nature reserve; here can been found growing oriental beech, Turkish nut-trees, chestnut, yew, lilac, Cauldrons tulips, figs, and dates. The Egyptian eagle, horn viper, and tortoise are also to be found in this area.

The Danube Cauldrons

By boat, on the Danube

On one of the banks of the Danube has been preserved the *Tabula Traiana*, carved into the rock by the Romans as they made their way into Dacia. At the point where the River Mraconia empties into the Danube there looms the imposing effigy of King Decebal (forty metres high and twenty-five metres wide), sculpted in 1998.

Romania's southern border holds a special charm, which is also created by the picturesque villages (*Belobreșca, Pojejena, Coronini, Liubovca, Berzasca, Dubova, Eșelnița*) threaded along the Danube, and by the unmistakable milieu of the ethnic communities in these parts, where Romanians, Serbs, Czechs and Bulgarians have been able to find the path to uniquely tranquil cohabitation.

The Roman roads also passed through the ancient Dacian settlement of *Drobeta*, which became an important military centre. Near the Danube can be found the ruins of the bridge built between 103 and 105 AD by the celebrated Apollodoros of Damascus.

On the Island of Șimian near Drobeta-Turnu Severin are housed some of the fourteenth century fortifications from the Island of Ada Kaleh, which was covered by the waters of the Danube after the construction of the Iron Gates Dam.

Băile Herculane

Here we are close to the *Banat*, a province that is especially privileged in its natural setting. The borders of this south-western region of Romania are formed by the Meridional Carpathians, the Danube and the Tisa and Mureș rivers. In this zone, the climate is much milder than in the rest of the country, with palpable Mediterranean influences.

On the *Cernea Valley* there is a marvellous spa resort – *Băile Herculane*, first attested in 153 AD. Around the mineral springs of this area, the Romans built thermal baths (*Ad aquas Herculis sacras*), whose ruins are still visible today. The statue of Hercules – the patron of the resort – made from cannon iron, was donated to the town in 1871 by Duke Karl.

Those who wish to enjoy the spell of the mountains need only head for the spa resort of *Semenic*, situated at an altitude of 1,400 metres on the Semenic Plateau. Here can also be found modern ski slopes.

8) Northern Oltenia

The region of northern Oltenia can not be taken in at just one glance. In order truly to get to know Oltenia, you must visit its countless monasteries and hermitages, its resorts with "miracle-working waters", its villages with ancient wooden churches. Here and there, you will come across caves, gorges and ravines...

The revelations of the ancient Dacian River *Alutus* (known as the Olt nowadays) are many. Following its course, we are confronted by ancient vestiges or monasteries and hermitages that preserve a mediaeval atmosphere. Near the Olt are preserved the traces of a chain of Roman forts, called the *Limes Alutanus*, which advance towards the Danube. We discover many architectural wonders in this region: the Cozia Monastery of Mircea the Old, the Tismana Monastery of Nicodim the Monk, the Hurez Monastery of Constantin Brâncoveanu, the Bistrița of the Craiovești boyars, Polovragi, a splendid example of Brâncoveanu architecture, the Monastery from a Single Tree, the Arnota and Govora of Matei Basarb, Frăsinei, which follows the *typikon* of the monks of Athos. In isolated corners there hide the hermitages, grottoes and cells of the hermits and monks who chose to withdraw into the wilderness: Turnu, Stânișoara, Ostrov, Bradu, Iezeru, Pahomie, Mamu, Dobrușa, Păpușa, Lainici, Locurele, Săcelu, Pătrunsa, Fedeleșoiu, Cornetu.

Oltenian dance

Here are preserved constructions named *cule*, which can also be found on the plains of Latin countries like Italy, Spain and France. A *culă* is a fortified dwelling, built by the great boyars for protection against incursions by armed bands of Turks who, in the eighteenth century, crossed the Danube from the Ottoman garrisons in Bulgaria. In time, the *cule* at Greceanu, Duca, Bujoreni, Poenaru, Cornoiu, and Crăsnaru have become tourist rather than strategic objectives on the map of Oltenia.

In the subterranean world beneath Oltenia have been identified more than two thousand forms of karst relief. The Cave of the Women, Polovragi Cave, Topolnița Cave, and the Cave of the Bats are the most well known. Truly spectacular are the Bistrița, Olteț and Jiu Gorges. At Costești (Vâlcea County) can be admired the "growing stones", as the local peasants call them. The Trovanți Museum contains strange formations, some reaching ten metres, mainly consisting of petrified silex, dating from the Superior Miocene Age. At Ponoare (Mehedinț County) can be found the *Bridge of God*, a karst formation unique in Romania. This huge vault remained standing after the walls of a large cave collapsed. Also unique in Romania is the lilac forest at Ponoare, a botanical reserve situated four kilometres from Baia de Arama. Year after year, in the first half of May, there is a lilac festival in the locality. The natural reserve of chestnuts and Turkish nut-tree at Tismana marks the perimeter of Mediterranean climatic influence.

Horezu pottery

The Călimănești-Căciulata resort

Oltenia is a region of very well known spa resorts: *Olănești, Căciulata, Călimănești, Govora, Voineasa.*

Traditions are still alive in Oltenia. Houses are built according to the old architectural models; there are wayside crosses at wells and crossroads, and even crosses carved into the trunk of trees. At Horezu can be found the most representative centre of traditional pottery. Every year, during the period from 3 to 5 June, the *Hurez Cockerel* Fair takes place. Horezu pottery is remarkable for its stylisation and its multiple symbols, using a distinctive technique for the modelling and the distribution of colours. Currently, there are more than one hundred traditional craftsmen living in Horezu. In Oltenia, a number of ancient pastoral festivals are still celebrated: the bringing of the sheep from the mountain, at Baia de Fier, on the third Sunday in September; the taking of the sheep into the mountains, at Novaci, in the month of May; Nedeia at Polovragi.

The lode of Oltenian tradition can be uncovered even in the work of Constantin Brâncuși, regarded as one of the greatest modern sculptors. Travellers to Târgu Jiu can admire four masterpieces by Brâncuși: *the Table of Silence, the Avenue of Chairs, the Gate of the Kiss, and the Column of the Infinite.*

9) The Apuseni Mountains

Travelling through the "stone citadel" of the Apuseni Mountains we are enveloped by the mythic atmosphere of the world's beginnings, for here we are traversing places that are just as pristine and wild as they were on the first day of creation. We are in the Land of the Moți – the kingdom of heights and freedom.

The traditions and customs of the Moți have a rare savour. The Maidens' Market at Mount Găina, an ancient fair, has already captured all Romanians; year after year, on the Sunday nearest the feast of St Elijah, thousands of people from all over the land perform the sacred ritual of ascending the slope to the grove situated at 1,467 metres, at the summit of the mountain. Whoever comes to this fair will never forget the sounds of the alpenhorn greeting the sunrise, the sprightly or slow rhythms of the matchless traditional dances, the legends of the golden hen...

The culture of woodcarving has been preserved intact here, at the heart of the mountains. The houses and churches of the Moți are just as beautiful in their simplicity as those of Maramureș folk. In some houses in the Apuseni Mountains, the locals display miniature collections of traditional art, which, in their way, tell the "history of wood". The Museum of Ethnography and Popular Art at Lupșa recreates, at another level, the same search for traditional values.

The Maidens Market on Mount Găina (1,467 m)

In the land of the Moți, Apuseni Mountains

If you come to the Apuseni Mountains, you must traverse the Arieș Valley – the river of gold- and see the Turda, Galbena and Someșul Cald gorges, and admire the Ponor Forts, with the Living Flame Glacier, and the Ruginoasa Pit. This is a karst realm: the numerous gorges (Râmeți, Aiud, Ampoița, Galda, Vălișoara) give the Apuseni a distinctive aspect. The Padiș Plateau, with its thirteen chasms, is, indisputably, a magnet for day-trippers. Here can be found strange formations, such as Snails Hill, a portion of seabed that has preserved millions of fossilised shells, or Detunata Goală, a rock formed by the solidification of volcanic lava. Four hundred caves hollow out the depths of the Apuseni: the Scărișoara Glacier, the Cave of the Bears, the Rădeasa Citadel, the Meziad Cave, Huda lui Papară and others.

The Transfăgărășan high altitude highway

10) The Transfăgărășan Highway (DN 7C)

The Transfăgărășan is an imposing high altitude highway, ninety kilometres long, which traverses the crest of the Făgăraș Mountains, the highest massif in Romania. It links the provinces of Muntenia (Argeș County) and Transylvania (Sibiu County). The dizzying hairpin bends of the Transfăgărășan are enough to unnerve any motorist. In any case, the recommended speed on this highway, which climbs to 2,000 metres, is 40 kilometres per hour. Since the snow persists for a long time at this altitude, the road, which, be warned, has no parapets, is closed from the end of October until June.

A journey along this highway takes us through breathtakingly beautiful places. We pass by the Bâlea Glacial Lake (2,034 m altitude), the Vidraru Reservoir, through the Capra, Bâlea and Cârtișoara glacial valleys. Along this one highway, we encounter – if you can believe it – no fewer than 27 viaducts and bridges and 550 smaller bridges. At Lake Bâlea, the Transfăgărășan passes through the longest tunnel in Romania (887 metres).

11) The Neamț region

Neamț is the region with the greatest density of monasteries and hermitages in the country. In effect, there is not a single mountain – for this is a mountainous region – without a hermitage or monastery. The perimeter in which can be found the Neamț, Secu, Sihăstria, Sihla, Agapia, and Văratec monasteries constitutes the true spiritual heart of Neamț.

Piatra-Neamț, the county seat, is one of the main departure points for excursions into this Moldavian region. In the city, attested from the fourteenth century, we can visit the *Museum of Neolithic Cucuteni Art* (Ștefan cel Mare Street, no. 3), which holds an archaeological collection that is unique in all of Europe. More than three hundred ceramic pieces are exhibited, belonging to the oldest Neolithic culture in Europe (sixth-third centuries BC): the *Ring-dances* from Frumușica and Drăgușeni, the *Thinker* from Târpești, *the Assembly of the Gods, the Vase with Columns* from Izvoare, as well as numerous anthropomorphic and zoomorphic statuettes. Cucuteni culture is celebrated for its ceramics decorated with spiral circle and meander motifs, the colours used being white, red and black. On a plateau in the centre of the city are still preserved some of the buildings of the former princely court, erected by Stephen the Great: the *Church of St John*, the belfry, cellars.

The church of the old princely court (15th century) at Piatra-Neamț

The Church of Neamț Monastery

Not far from the town we can visit: *Bistrița Monastery*, founded ante 1407 by Prince Alexandru the Good, the *Bisericani Monastery* (fifteenth century), *Pângărați Monastery*, founded in 1461, during the time of Stephen the Great, by Simion the monk from the Bistrița Monastery, Războieni Monastery, built by Stephen the Great in 1496.

Situated 44 km from the municipality of Piatra-Neamț, by the Ozana (Neamț) River, *Târgu-Neamț* owes its development to the construction of a strong citadel on the Pleșu Summit, between 1374 and 1391, during the time of Petru Mușat the First. Near the locality of Vânători Neamț can be found the *Dragoș Vodă* Reservation for aurochs and Carpathian fauna (11,500 hectares).

Roman, an ancient mediaeval market town, mentioned in documents as early as 1392, is thought to have been founded by Roman Mușat the First. In 1408, during the reign of Alexandru the Good, Roman became an episcopal see. The *episcopal cathedral* (no. 5 Alexandru the Good Street), dedicated to the *Blessed Parascheva*, was constructed between 1542 and 1550 by Petru Rareș and his son, Iliaș, on the site of a church from the time of Petru Mușat. The *house of Done the Dvornik* (no. 2 Agnita Street), with its classical facades and baroque interiors, currently houses the *Sergiu Celibidache Music School*. The great conductor was born in this house in 1912.

The town of *Bicaz*, twenty-eight kilometres from the town of Piatra-Neamț (on the DN 15), in the foothills of the Ceahlau Mountains, at the confluence of the Bistrița and Bicaz rivers, developed especially after the construction of the Izvorul Muntelui/Bicaz Dam and Reservoir, which stretches for thirty-five kilometres. Those who come to Bicaz should not miss the *Bicaz Gorge*, situated 27 km south-west. This sector of the Bicaz Valley, through which the waters pass through the Hășmaș Massif of the Carpathian Mountains, for a length of eight kilometres, is particularly spectacular. We recommend that you take the route between Bicazu Ardelean and Lacul Roșu, along the DN 12 C (which links Bicaz to Gheorgheni). After the spectacle of the Bicaz Gorge, you will have occasion to discover an interesting lake. *Red Lake*, with a surface area of thirteen hectares and a depth of ten and a half metres, formed in 1837, after a landslide on the north-west slope of Mount Ghilcoș, caused by heavy rainfall, blocked the Verescheu (Roșu) Valley. At the surface of this natural reservoir can still be seen the trunks of the firs that were flooded at the time. Near Lacul Roșu, at an altitude of 983 m, there in time developed the Lacul Roșu resort (Harghita County), equipped with three ski slopes, one of which is 2,400 metres long. The resort, just three kilometres from the Bicaz Gorge, is considered a wonderful departure point for hiking in the surrounding mountains.

Izvorul Muntelui (Bicaz) Lake

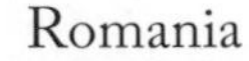

The Ceahlău Massif

The *Ceahlău Massif* is remarkable especially for its massivity and the presence of a particularly picturesque ruiniform relief (steep drops, towers, thresholds, crags). The ascent of the Ocolașu Mare (1,907 m), Toaca (1,904 m), Panaghia (1,900 m) and Ocolașu Mic (1,712 m) summits is a true challenge for all. The Duruitoarea watefall, which gave its name to the Durău monastery and resort, is one of the most accessible points of the Ceahlău. The waters of this cataract, fed by the Rupturi Stream, at an altitude of 1,021 metres, fall from a height of approximately twenty-five metres. It is possible to stay overnight in the heart of the mountains, at the *Fântânele, Dochia* and *Izvorul Muntelui* chalets. In Durău, a resort situated at 800 m altitude – the main access route to the Ceahlău Massif – there are numerous hotels, of various categories. Winter sports enthusiasts will find here a three hundred-metre ski slope.

Romania – Urban Landmarks

Bucharest, the capital of Romania, is a true European city, overwhelming in the brilliance of its edifices: *the Palace of the National Savings Bank, the Romanian Athenaeum, the George Enescu Museum (the Cantacuzino Palace), the Municipality of Bucharest Museum of History (the Șuțu Palace), the National Museum of History, the Military Club, the National Museum of Art (the former Royal Palace), the Central University Library (the former Palace of the Carol I University Foundation), the Cotroceni Palace, the Palace of the Ministry of Agriculture, the Palace of the Patriarchate, the Știrbei Palace, the University, the Romanian Opera.*

The first documentary attestation of Bucharest dates from 1459, in a document issued by Vlad the Impaler, who had established his residence in this citadel on the banks of the Dâmbovița. The historic centre of the city preserves the ruins of the princely court (the *Old Court*) and the princely church (dedicated to the feast of the Annunciation), built between 1558 and 1559. After it became the permanent capital of the Romanian Land in 1659, the city of Bucharest began to expand; the crafts flourished, numerous foreign merchants settled here, inns were built (such as *Manuc's Inn*), and also churches (*Zlătari, Stavropoleos, St George*), schools (*the St Sava Academy*), hospitals (*Colțea Hospital, Pantelimon Hospital*).

At the beginning of the twentieth century, elegant Bucharest was nicknamed "the Little Paris". Many of its monumental buildings, constructed in the nineteenth century, display the influence of French architectural style. Today, the dynamic life of this fascinating metropolis, in step with the times, unfolds different charms, which are ever waiting to be discovered along its bustling streets flanked with eclectic buildings.

Calea Victoriei, Bucharest

The Palace of Parliament (named the *House of the People* during the communist period) is a colossal edifice, the second largest in the world after the Pentagon. Eighty-four metres high and with six thousand rooms, covering a built surface area of 330,000 square metres, the building was constructed on Spirii Hill between 1984 and 1989. Dictator Nicolae Ceausescu intended to establish here the presidential residence, the Central Committee of the Communist Party and a number of ministries. The Palace of Parliament contains more than four hundred offices, and dozens of conference and reception rooms. The most sumptuous of these is the Hall of Union (2,200 square metres), with a seating capacity of one thousand, splendidly illuminated by a chandelier with seven thousand light bulbs, which weighs three tons. Today, the building house the Romanian Parliament, the International Conference Centre and the National Museum of Contemporary Art. In front of the Palace stretches the vast Constitution Square, where concerts and performances are held.

The Palace of Parliament

The palace of Constantin Brâncoveanu, Mogoșoaia

The *Cișmigiu Gardens* in the centre of Bucharest arc the oldest park in the city. They were first laid out in 1845. The current configuration of the park is the work of German landscape gardeners Karl Wilhelm Meyer and Fr. Rebhuhn. For the inhabitants of Bucharest, it is a favourite place for walks. The floral arrangement, the rare trees and shrubs, the lake, which offers boating, the fountains and sculptures all make up the charm of Cișmigiu.

The *Museum of the Village*, founded in 1936 by sociologist Dimitrie Gusti, is an open-air ethnographic museum, occupying ten hectares of Herăstrău Park. Here you can see 272 traditional rural buildings from all over Romania.

The city is surrounded by forests and a chain of lakes, around which have grown up recreational areas, wonderful places to spend the weekend: *Herăstrău Lake, Snagov Lake and Forest, Băneasa Forest, and Căldărușani, Pasărea, Cernica and Mogoșoaia Lakes*. Nearby there are old monasteries (*Cernica, Pasărea, Căldărușani, Snagov*) and princely palaces (*Mogoșoaia Palace*, built in 1702 by Constantin Brâncoveanu, housing the *Museum of Brâncoveanu Feudal Art*).

Cluj-Napoca is a genuinely European city. Always open to the new, Cluj has kept pace with the times. It is one of the most important cultural centres of Romania. Here there are nine institutes of higher education, with forty-nine faculties, and numerous research institutes.

The history of Cluj, like that of other Trasylvanian cities, goes back far in time. The former Dacian citadel of Napoca became, during Roman domination, a *municipium* and then *colonia*. In 1316 it gained the status of *civitas*. Of the fortifications built after 1407, the Firemen's and Builders' Towers have been preserved, as well as the Bastions of the Tailors, Clothiers and Cobblers, fragments of the defensive wall and the fortified citadel.

The centre of the city is dominated by the Roman Catholic Cathedral of *St Michael*, built in the gothic style during the fourteenth and fifteenth centuries, with an eighty-metre neo-gothic tower constructed in the nineteenth century. Nearby, there is a large statue of Matei Corvin on horseback, made in 1902 by artist János Fadrusz.

The National Theatre, Cluj-Napoca

Architectural and sculptural monuments in Cluj-Napoca

Cluj has a long list of tourist attractions. The traveller will require a number of days to see all that the city has to offer: the Church of the Benedictine Monastery (1222), the Mănăștur-Calvaria Church (thirteenth century); the Reformed Church (1486-1494), in front of which there is an equestrian statue of *St George slaying the dragon*, sculpted in 1373 by Martin and Gheorghe; the Jesuits' Church, the Orthodox Cathedral, with a cupola inspired by that of *Hagia Sophia*; the baroque palace that belonged to Count Banffy (1773-1785), which houses the Cluj Museum of Art; the Teleki Palace, built in the neo-classical style between 1790 and 1795; the National Theatre and Romanian Opera, inaugurated in 1919; the Council Palace; the fifteenth century house of Matei Corvin; the house where Franz Liszt lived in 1846; the *Babeș-Bolyai* University; the Botanical Gardens; the open-air Ethnographic Museum on Hoia Hill; and much more.

The Timişoara Opera House

Timişoara is the Romanian town which is said most to bear the imprint of the baroque: the old Town Hall (1731-1734), the Roman Catholic Episcopal Palace (1743-1752), the Palace of the Prefecture (1754), the *St Catherine* Roman Catholic Church (1752-1755), the *St George* Serbian Church (1745-1755).

In 1307, Carol I Robert de Anjou, the King of Hungary, decided to build a fortress in this settlement, which is mentioned in documents from the year 1212 as *Castrum Timisiensis* (*Castrum regium Themes*). The fortress would be rebuilt in the fifteenth century by Iancu of Hunedoara. The Castle of the Huniazi, which now houses the Museum of Banat History, is one of the main attractions of Timişoara.

Between 1552 and 1716, the city was the residence of the Timişoara Pasha, and between 1716 and 1918 it was part of the Austro-Hungarian Empire. Under Austrian rule, dykes were built along the River Bega and beautiful baroque edifices were constructed. Since the end of the nineteenth century, Timişoara has been a modern city, with electricity and telephone networks, public transport etc.

There are a number of places which no visitor to Timișoara should miss seeing: the Roman Catholic Cathedral, built between 1736 and 1774 in the baroque style; the Dicasterial Palace (now the County Courts), with 350 rooms, built between 1850 and 1854 in the Renaissance style, after the Strozzi Palace in Florence; the Deschau Palace, built in the neo-classical style in 1735; and the imposing Orthodox Cathedral of the *Three Hierarchs* (1936-1946).

Iași, the city sited, like Rome, on seven hills, is, of course, "the heart of Moldavia". In Iași, there are numerous churches, monasteries and memorial houses, monuments, palaces and historic buildings.

Iași began to develop as a town in the fifteenth century, after the princes of Moldavia established their residence here. In the period between 1564 and 1859, when it was the capital of the province of Moldavia, many of the superb buildings of Iași were constructed.

The Monastery of the *Three Hierarchs* (1635-1639), founded by Vasile Lupu, combines elements of Moldavian and Walachian architecture. The rich exterior decoration, sculpted in stone, makes this church unique in Romania.

The Palace of Culture, Jassy

The Town Council and Black Church, Brașov

The *Church of St Nicolae*, built by Stephen the Great in 1491-1492, was formerly part of the princely court. It was here that the princes of Moldavia were anointed from the sixteenth century until 1859.

Other old churches of Iași: the Church of the Galata Monastery, built in 1576-1578 by Petru the Lame; the Church of the Golia Monastery, from the beginning of the sixteenth century, rebuilt by Vasile Lupu; the church of the Cetățuia Monastery (1668-1672), founded by Lord Gheorghe Duca; the church of the Frumoasa Monastery (1583-1586); the Roman Catholic Cathedral (the Franciscans' Church), built in 1782-1789; the Armenian-Gregorian Church (1395).

The neo-gothic edifice of the Palace of Culture, built on the site of the former princely court between 1907 and 1926 and designed by architect I.D. Bernidei, now houses a vast museum complex. The Palace of Prince Alexandru Ioan Cuza (1806) houses the Museum of Union. The House of Dosoftei (1677), where a printing press once operated, is now the Museum of Printing.

The Mihail Sturdza Palace (1834-1848), now the Conservatory, the Beldiman House (1819) and the Roset-Roznoveanu Palace (1832-1834) are testimonies to the former splendour of Iași.

Brașov, situated at the foot of the Tâmpa Mountain, is one of Romania's main tourist centres. The old centre of the city (*Council Square*), flanked by Renaissance-style, baroque and neo-classical buildings, is dominated by the celebrated *Black Church* (1384-1477), the largest gothic construction in Romania, with a facade adorned by numerous stone carvings. The interior of this church conceals many treasures: fifteenth century murals painted in the Renaissance style, more than a hundred oriental carpets, and a four-thousand pipe organ, thought to be the largest in Europe. The Bartholomew Church (thirteenth century) is in the early gothic style.

Many of the fortifications of the mediaeval city of Brașov (*Kronstadt*) have been preserved: sections of the city wall, the Ecaterina Gate, the Butchers' Tower, the Black Tower, and the Weavers', Ropers', Furriers', Clothiers' and Blacksmiths' Bastions.

The area around Brașov is one of the most visited tourist destinations in Romania. From here, we can set off on excursions to the Făgăraș, Rupea and Râșnov castles and the mediaeval castles at Bran, Racoș and Hoghiz.

The mountain resort of **Poiana Brașov**, above which looms the Postăvaru Massif, is just twelve kilometres away. Winter sports enthusiasts will find numerous ski slopes here.

By cable car in Poiana Brașov

The Casino at Constanța

Constanța, the ancient Greek colony of *Tomis* (seventh century BC), is Romania's largest Black Sea port. The current name of the city (*Constantia*) was adopted in the fourth century AD after the Emperor Constantine built a district here – named *Constantiniana*. From Roman times, there have been preserved an emporium, with an impressive polychrome mosaic, preserved intact for a surface area of 2,000 square metres. The Genoese established a colony in Constanța in the thirteenth century. They built a lighthouse here, which can still be seen today.

During the reign of Carol I, the port was modernised by engineer Anghel Saligny. In the same period, numerous hotels were built, as well as the imposing Art Nouveau Casino (1909).

It is impossible not to fall under the spell of Constanța's cosmopolitan atmosphere. Here we can find mosques in the Moorish style, Armenian churches, Roman Catholic cathedrals, Romanian Orthodox churches, and Bulgarian and Greek churches.

Sibiu, a modern western city, still preserves the traces of the flourishing mediaeval burg of former times and the Viennese baroque buildings constructed after Transylvania came under Hapsburg administration in 1699.

Sibiu (*Cibinum*) was first attested in 1191 and later renamed *Hermannstadt*. In the Middle Ages it was fortified with massive red brick walls – whence it is also called the *Red Citadel* – and defensive towers and bastions. The Gros, Soldisch and Haller Bastions, and the Council, Joiners', Arquebusiers', Potters', and Tanners' Towers have been preserved. It was one of the main trading centres of the time. The Sibiu guilds sold their goods as far away as in Vienna, Prague, Leipzig and Danzig.

The fourteenth century Evangelical Church, a monument representative of the Transylvanian gothic style, with its seventy-three metre high tower, houses a beautiful baroque organ, constructed in 1671 by a Slovak master craftsman. The Minorite Church (thirteenth century) and Ursuline Church (1479), the church of the former Franciscan Monastery (1716) and the Orthodox Cathedral of the *Holy Trinity*, built after the model of *Hagia Sophia* in Constantinople, are all landmarks of Sibiu.

Make sure that you cross the Bridge of Lies (*Lugenbrucke*), the first cast iron bridge in Romania (1859): according to legend, it will collapse on the spot if you tell a lie.

The symbol of the city is, however, the Brukenthal Palace, built in 1778-1788 by the Governor of Transylvania, Baron Samuel Bruckenthal.

The historic centre of Sibiu

Oradea, the largest town in the Romanian province of Crișana, has become in time an important commercial centre. Its development has been favoured by its position at the intersection of the roads that link West, Central and South East Europe. Situated just twelve kilometres from the border, Oradea is the main gateway to Romania from Western Europe.

The period of Austrian domination was beneficial in every respect for Oradea. It was then that the Orthodox Cathedral of the *Dormition of the Mother of God* was built. It is known as the *church with the moon* (since the steeple houses a clock with a mechanism that also shows the phases of the moon) and is characterised by its baroque and neo-classical architecture. Also from this period date the Roman Catholic Cathedral of the *Virgin Mary*, one of the most impressive baroque monuments in the country, the Roman Catholic Episcopal Palace, the Roman catholic Church of *St Ladislas*, the Synagogue, the Palace of the Chamber of Commerce, the Town Hall, the Theatre, the Palace of Justice, and the Apollo, Ulman and the Black Eagle Palaces.

In the immediate vicinity of the city (8-10 km) there are two renowned spa resorts: *Băile Felix* and *Băile 1 Mai.*

The Black Eagle Palace, on the banks of the Crișul Repede River, Oradea

Craiova Town Hall

Craiova is, from all points of view, the centre of Oltenia. It is undoubtedly one of the most beautiful cities in Romania.

Although it is attested only as late as 1475, the history of Craiova goes back much further. In the fourth century BC the Dacian citadel of *Pelendava* was located here. Since the fifteenth century it has been the administrative capital of Oltenia, and has never ceased to develop.

The Princely Church was founded in 1651-1652 by Matei Basarab. Destroyed by the earthquake of 1838, it was rebuilt by French architect Lecomte du Noüy. It is now the Metropolitan Cathedral of Oltenia. The Church of *St Elijah* (1720) has murals by Gheorghe Tattarescu, one of the great Romanian painters, who lived in the nineteenth century.

Some of the civic buildings of Craiova may be considered veritable historic monuments: the Glogoveanu House, the Jianu House, the former Palace of Justice (now the seat of the University), the Administrative Palace.

The Art Museum, housed in a palace built in 1896 and designed by French architect Paul Gottereau, preserves six sculptures by Constantin Brâncuși. The Baniei House, built in 1699 by Constantin Brâncoveanu, houses the Museum of Ethnography and Traditional Art.

The Romanescu Park, laid out in 1900-1903 to the plans of French architect Emile Redont, covers an area of ninety hectares.

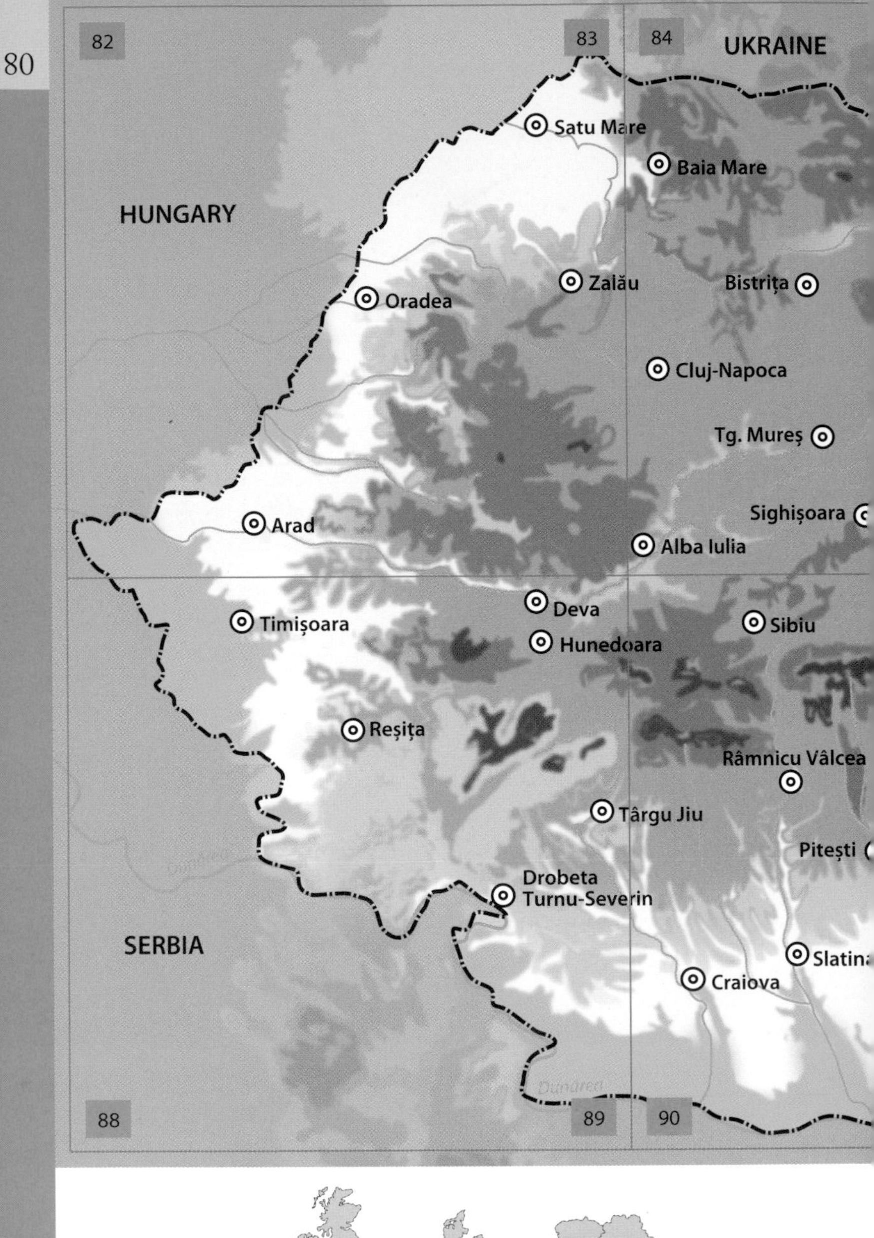
82
83
84
UKRAINE
Satu Mare
Baia Mare
HUNGARY
Zalău
Bistrița
Oradea
Cluj-Napoca
Tg. Mureș
Sighișoara
Arad
Alba Iulia
Deva
Timișoara
Sibiu
Hunedoara
Reșița
Râmnicu Vâlcea
Târgu Jiu
Pitești
Drobeta
Turnu-Severin
SERBIA
Slatina
Craiova
Dunărea
88
89
90

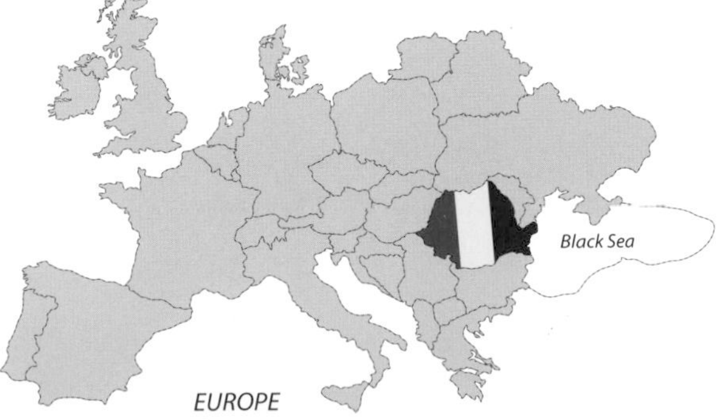
Black Sea
EUROPE

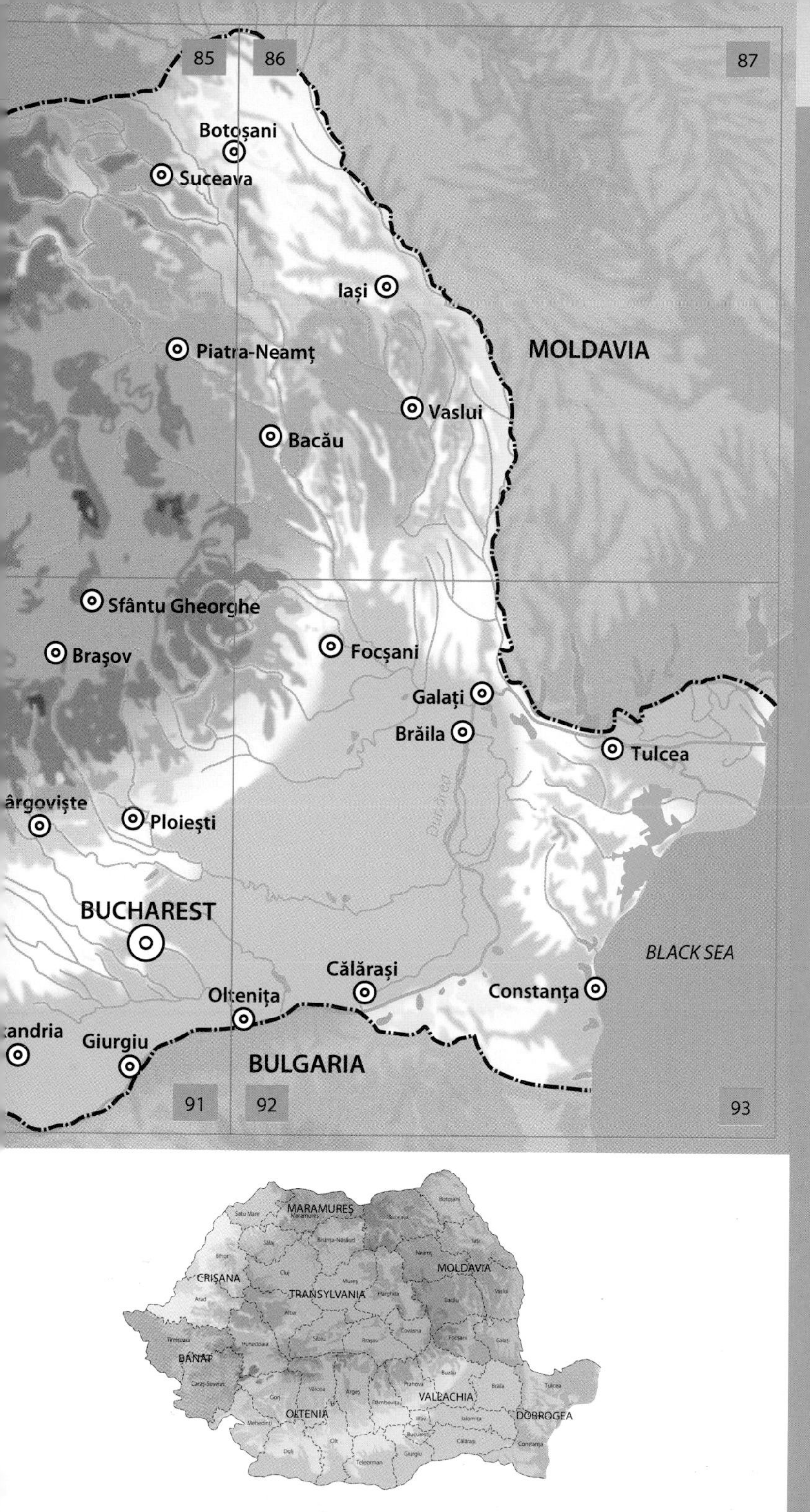

85
86
87
Botoșani
Suceava
Iași
Piatra-Neamț
MOLDAVIA
Vaslui
Bacău
Sfântu Gheorghe
Brașov
Focșani
Galați
Brăila
Tulcea
Dunărea
âргoviște
Ploiești
BUCHAREST
BLACK SEA
Călărași
Constanța
Oltenița
xandria
Giurgiu
BULGARIA
91
92
93
MARAMUREȘ
CRIȘANA
TRANSYLVANIA
MOLDAVIA
BANAT
VALLACHIA
OLTENIA
DOBROGEA

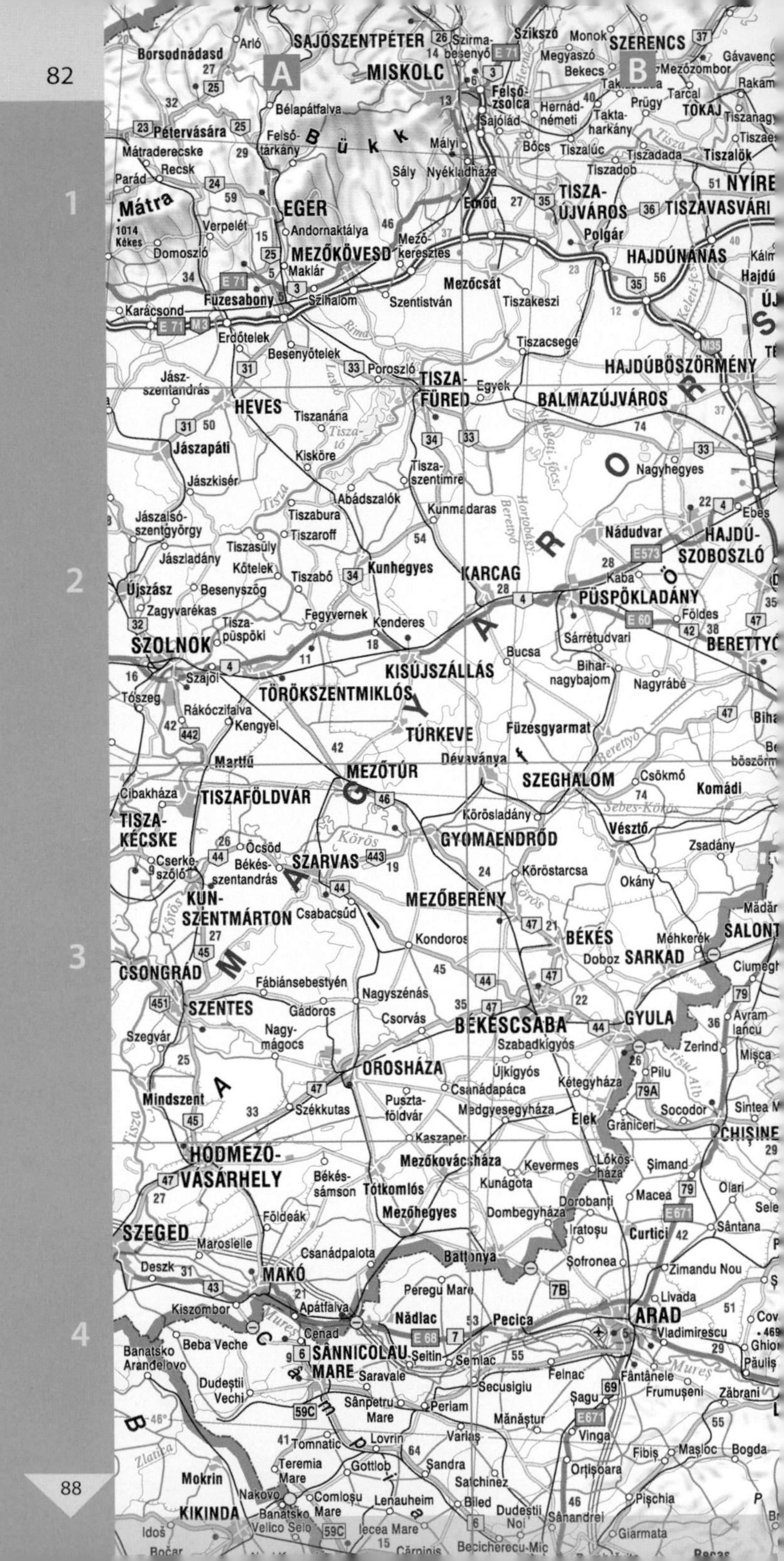
A
B
1
2
3
4
Borsodnádasd
Arló
SAJÓSZENTPÉTER
Szirma-besenyő
Szikszó
Monok
SZERENCS
Gávavencsellő
MISKOLC
Megyaszó
Bekecs
Mezőzombor
Rakamaz
Felső-zsolca
Hernád-németi
Prügy
Tarcal
TOKAJ
Bélapátfalva
Sajólád
Takta-harkány
Pétervására
Felső-tárkány
B ü k k
Mályi
Bőcs
Tiszalúc
Tiszadada
Tiszalök
Mátraderecske
Recsk
Sály
Nyékládháza
Tiszadob
Parád
NYÍREGYHÁZA
Mátra
EGER
Emőd
TISZA-ÚJVÁROS
TISZAVASVÁRI
1014 Kékes
Verpelét
Andornaktálya
Mező-keresztes
Polgár
Domoszló
MEZŐKÖVESD
HAJDÚNÁNÁS
Maklár
Mezőcsát
Füzesabony
Szihalom
Szentistván
Tiszakeszi
Karácsond
Erdőtelek
Rima
Besenyőtelek
Tiszacsege
Jász-szentandrás
Poroszló
TISZA-FÜRED
Egyek
HAJDÚBÖSZÖRMÉNY
HEVES
BALMAZÚJVÁROS
Tiszanána
Tisza-tó
Jászapáti
Kisköre
Tisza-szentimre
Nagyhegyes
Jászkisér
Abádszalók
Kunmadaras
Hortobágy
Jászalsó-szentgyörgy
Tiszabura
Tiszaroff
Nádudvar
HAJDÚ-SZOBOSZLÓ
Ebes
Tiszasüly
Jászladány
Kőtelek
Tiszabő
Kunhegyes
KARCAG
Kaba
Újszász
Besenyszög
PÜSPÖKLADÁNY
Zagyvarékas
Fegyvernek
Kenderes
Földes
Tisza-püspöki
SZOLNOK
Sárrétudvari
BERETTYÓÚJFALU
Bucsa
Szajol
KISÚJSZÁLLÁS
Bihar-nagybajom
Nagyrábé
Tószeg
TÖRÖKSZENTMIKLÓS
Rákóczifalva
Kengyel
TÚRKEVE
Füzesgyarmat
Martfű
Dévaványa
MEZŐTÚR
SZEGHALOM
Csökmő
Cibakháza
TISZAFÖLDVÁR
Komádi
TISZA-KÉCSKE
Körösladány
Vésztő
Sebes-Körös
Öcsöd
GYOMAENDRŐD
Zsadány
Cserke-szőlő
Békés-szentandrás
SZARVAS
Köröstarcsa
Okány
KUN-SZENTMÁRTON
Csabacsűd
MEZŐBERÉNY
Mădăras
SALONTA
Kondoros
BÉKÉS
Méhkerék
CSONGRÁD
Doboz
SARKAD
Ciumeghiu
Fábiánsebestyén
Nagyszénás
SZENTES
Gádoros
Csorvás
BÉKÉSCSABA
GYULA
Avram Iancu
Szegvár
Nagy-mágocs
Szabadkígyós
Zerind
Mișca
OROSHÁZA
Újkígyós
Pilu
Csanádapáca
Kétegyháza
Mindszent
Székkutas
Puszta-földvár
Medgyesegyháza
Elek
Grăniceri
Socodor
Sintea Mare
Kaszaper
CHIȘINEU-CRIȘ
HÓDMEZŐ-VÁSÁRHELY
Mezőkovácsháza
Kevermes
Lőkös-háza
Șimand
Békés-sámson
Tótkomlós
Kunágota
Macea
Olari
Dorobanți
Földeák
Mezőhegyes
Dombegyháza
Sântana
SZEGED
Iratoșu
Curtici
Maroslele
Csanádpalota
Battonya
Șofronea
Deszk
MAKÓ
Zimandu Nou
Peregu Mare
Livada
Kiszombor
Apátfalva
Nădlac
Pecica
ARAD
Cenad
Vladimirescu
Banatsko Aranđelovo
Beba Veche
SÂNNICOLAU MARE
Seltin
Semlac
Felnac
Fântânele
Mureș
Saravale
Frumușeni
Zăbrani
Dudeștii Vechi
Secusigiu
Șagu
Sânpetru Mare
Perjam
Mănăștur
Vinga
Tomnatic
Lovrin
Variaș
Fibiș
Maşloc
Bogda
Teremia Mare
Gottlob
Șandra
Orțișoara
Mokrin
Satchinez
Nakovo
Comloșu Mare
Lenauheim
Biled
Pișchia
KIKINDA
Banatsko Veliko Selo
Dudeștii Noi
Sânandrei
Iecea Mare
Giarmata
Becicherecu Mic
Idoš
M A G Y A R O R S Z Á G
C â m p i a
Zlatica
Körös
Tisza
Berettyó

88

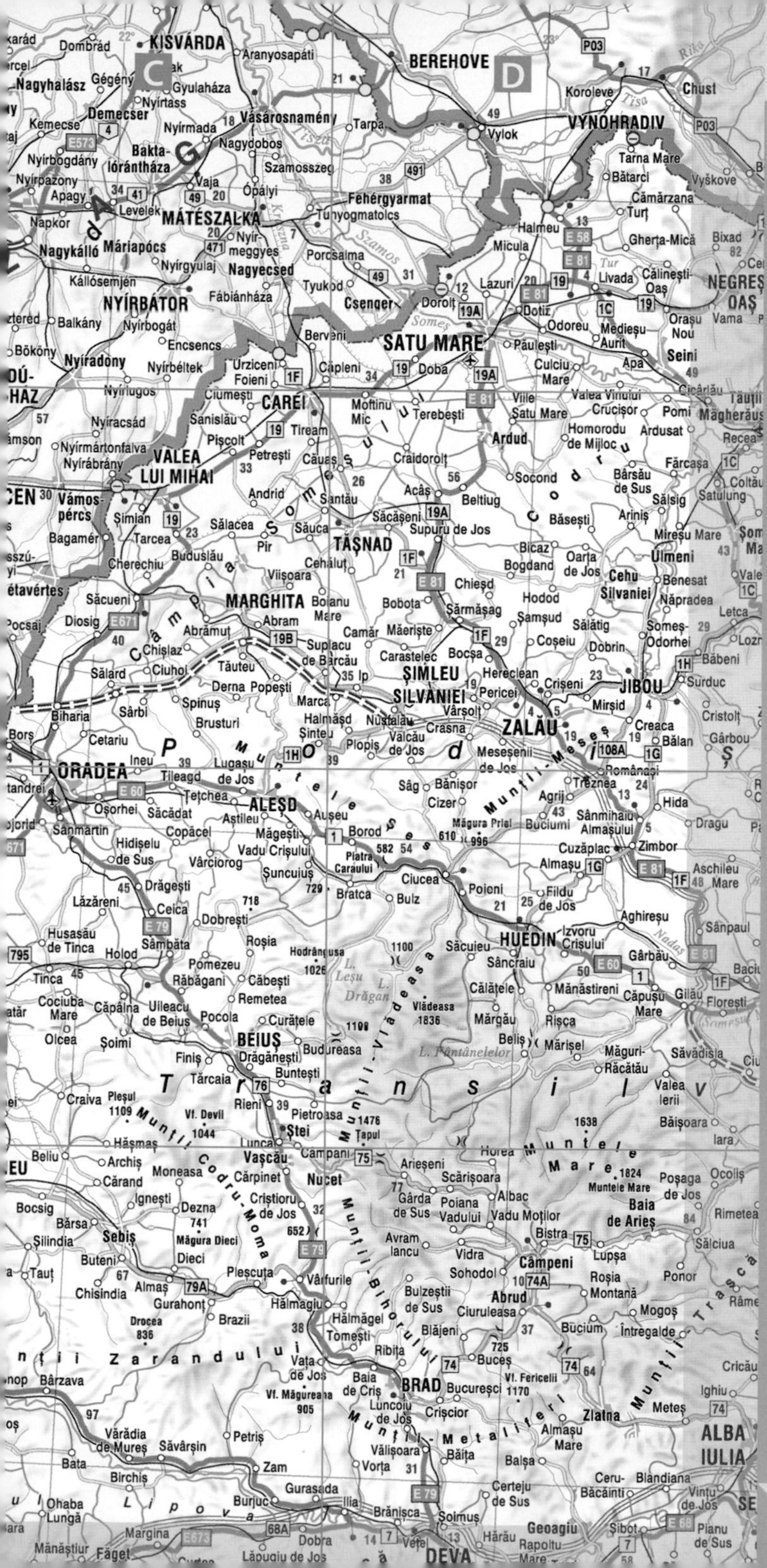

KISVÁRDA
Dombrád
Aranyosapáti
BEREHOVE
Chust
Nagyhalász
Gégény
Gyulaháza
Nyírtass
Koroleve
Tisa
Demecser
Kemecse
Nyírmada
Vásárosnamény
Tarpa
Vylok
VYNOHRADIV
Nagydobos
Nyírbogdány
Bakta-lórántháza
Szamosszeg
Tarna Mare
Bătarci
Vyškove
Nyírpazony
Apagy
Vaja
Ópályi
Fehérgyarmat
Cămărzana
Napkor
Levelek
MÁTÉSZALKA
Tunyogmatolcs
Turț
Halmeu
Nagykálló
Máriapócs
Nyírmeggyes
Porcsalma
Micula
Gherța-Mică
Bixad
Nyírgyulaj
Nagyecsed
Szamos
Kállósemjén
Tyukod
Lazuri
Livada
Călinești-Oaș
NEGREȘTI OAȘ
NYÍRBÁTOR
Fábiánháza
Csenger
Dorolț
Dotiz
Odoreu
Mediașu Aurit
Orașu Nou
Vama
Balkány
Nyírbogát
Encsencs
Berveni
Someș
SATU MARE
Păulești
Seini
Bököny
Nyíradony
Nyírbéltek
Urziceni Foieni
Căpleni
Doba
Culciu Mare
Apa
Cicârlău
Nyírlugos
Ciumești
CAREI
Moftinu Mic
Terebești
Viile Satu Mare
Valea Vinului
Crucișor
Pomi
Tăuții Măgherăuș
Nyíracsád
Sanislău
Tiream
Ardud
Homorodu de Mijloc
Ardusat
Recea
Nyírmártonfalva
Nyírábrány
Pișcolt
VALEA LUI MIHAI
Petrești
Căuaș
Craidorolț
Bârsău de Sus
Fărcașa
Coltău
Vámospércs
Șimian
Andrid
Santău
Acâș
Socond
Sălsig
Satulung
Bagamér
Tarcea
Sălacea
Săuca
Săcășeni
Supuru de Jos
Beltiug
Bășești
Ariniș
Mireșu Mare
Șomcuta Mare
Cherechiu
Buduslău
Pir
TĂȘNAD
Cehăluț
Bicaz
Bogdand
Oarța de Jos
Cehu Silvaniei
Ulmeni
Benesat
Viișoara
Chieșd
Hodod
Năpradea
Létavértes
Săcueni
MARGHITA
Bobota
Bozanu Mare
Șărmășag
Șamșud
Sălătig
Someș-Odorhei
Letca
Pocsaj
Diosig
Abrămuț
Abram
Camăr
Măeriște
Coșeiu
Dobrin
Băbeni
Chișlaz
Suplacu de Barcău
Carastelec
Bocșa
Sălard
Ciuhoi
Tăuteu
Ip
ȘIMLEU SILVANIEI
Hereclean
Crișeni
JIBOU
Surduc
Derna
Popești
Marca
Pericei
Mirșid
Cristolț
Biharia
Sârbi
Spinuș
Halmășd
Nușfalău
Vârșolț
ZALĂU
Creaca
Gârbou
Borș
Brusturi
Șinteu
Crasna
Bălan
Cetariu
Plopiș
Vălcău de Jos
Meseșenii de Jos
ORADEA
Ineu
Lugașu de Jos
Tileagd
Sâg
Bănișor
Românași
Treznea
Hida
Țețchea
ALEȘD
Cizer
Agrij
Oșorhei
Săcădat
Aștileu
Aușeu
Măgura Priei
Buciumi
Sânmihaiu Almașului
Dragu
Sânmartin
Copăcel
Măgești
Borod
Cuzăplac
Zimbor
Hidișelu de Sus
Vadu Crișului
Piatra Craiului
Almașu
Aschileu Mare
Vârciorog
Șuncuiuș
Ciucea
Poieni
Fildu de Jos
Drăgești
Lăzăreni
Bratca
Bulz
Ceica
Dobrești
Aghireșu
Husasău de Tinca
Sâmbăta
Roșia
Hodrâncusa
Săcuieu
HUEDIN
Izvoru Crișului
Sânpaul
Holod
Pomezeu
Sâncraiu
Gârbău
Baciu
Tinca
Răbăgani
Căbești
L. Leșu
L. Drăgan
Călățele
Mănăstireni
Căpușu Mare
Gilău
Florești
Cociuba Mare
Căpâlna
Uileacu de Beiuș
Remetea
Vlădeasa
Mărgău
Rișca
Olcea
Pocola
Curățele
Șoimi
BEIUȘ
Drăgănești
Budureasa
Beliș
Mărișel
Măguri-Răcătău
Săvădisla
Finiș
Buntești
L. Fântânelelor
Tărcaia
Valea Ierii
Craiva
Pleșul
Rieni
Pietroasa
Vf. Devil
Țapul
Băișoara
Hășmaș
Lunca
Ștei
Iara
Beliu
Archiș
Vașcău
Câmpani
Horea
Moneasa
Cărpinet
Nucet
Arieșeni
Scărișoara
Posaga de Jos
Ocoliș
Cărand
Ignești
Cristioru de Jos
Gârda de Sus
Poiana Vadului
Albac
Vadu Moților
Muntele Mare
Baia de Arieș
Rimetea
Bocsig
Dezna
Bârsa
Măgura Dieci
Avram Iancu
Bistra
Sălciua
Șilindia
Sebiș
Dieci
Vidra
Câmpeni
Lupșa
Buteni
Sohodol
Tauț
Pleșcuța
Vârfurile
Roșia Montană
Ponor
Chisindia
Almaș
Gurahonț
Bulzeștii de Sus
Abrud
Mogoș
Râmeț
Drocea
Hălmagiu
Ciuruleasa
Hălmăgel
Brazii
Tomești
Blăjeni
Bucium
Întregalde
Ribița
Buceș
Vața de Jos
Cricău
Bârzava
Baia de Criș
BRAD
București
Vf. Fericelii
Ighiu
Vf. Măgureana
Luncoiu de Jos
Crișcior
Zlatna
Meteș
Vărădia de Mureș
Săvârșin
Petriș
Almașu Mare
ALBA IULIA
Bata
Zam
Vălișoara
Băița
Vorța
Balșa
Birchiș
Gurasada
Ceru-Băcăinți
Blandiana
Ohaba Lungă
Burjuc
Ilia
Certeju de Sus
Vințu de Jos
Brănișca
Șoimuș
Mănăștiur
Făget
Margina
Dobra
Lăpugiu de Jos
Veței
DEVA
Hărău
Geoagiu
Rapoltu Mare
Șibot
Pianu de Sus

Muntele Mare
Muntii Vlădeasa
Munții Bihorului
Munții Codru-Moma
Munții Metaliferi
Munții Trascău
Munții Zarandului
Munții Meseș
Munții Plopiș
Câmpia Someșului
Câmpia Crișurilor
Codru
Transilvania
Lipova

84
89

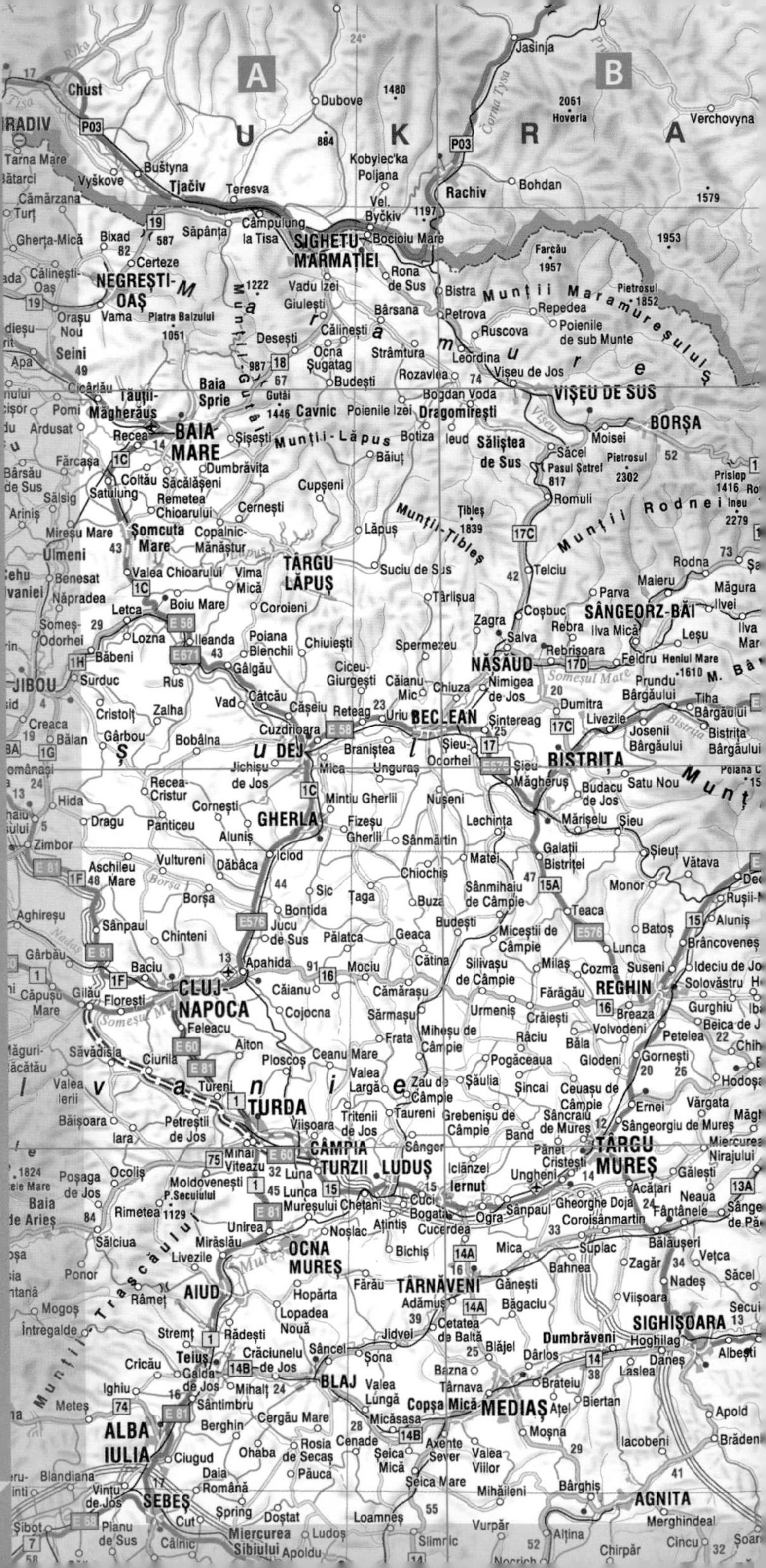

A B

U K R A

1 2 3 4

Chust
VINOHRADIV
P03
Tarna Mare
Bătarci
Vyškove
Buštyna
Tjačiv
Teresva
Dubove
1480
884
Kobylec'ka Poljana
Vel. Byčkiv
1197
Jasinja
Čorna Tysa
P03
Rachiv
Bohdan
2061 Hoverla
Verchovyna
1579
Cămărzana
Turț
Gherța-Mică
Bixad
82
19
587
Săpânța
Câmpulung la Tisa
SIGHETU MARMAȚIEI
Bocioiu Mare
1953
Farcău 1957
Pietrosul 1852
Călinești-Oaș
Certeze
NEGREȘTI-OAȘ
1222
Vadu Izei
Giulești
Rona de Sus
Bistra
Munții Maramureșului
Repedea
Poienile de sub Munte
Vama
Orașu Nou
Piatra Balzului 1051
Bârsana
Petrova
Călinești
Desești
Ruscova
Seini
49
Apa
987
18
Ocna Șugatag
Strâmtura
Leordina
Vișeu de Jos
Rozavlea
74
67
Budești
Baia Sprie
Gutâi 1446
Cicârlău
Tăuții-Măgherăuș
Pomi
Ardusat
Cavnic
Poienile Izei
Bogdan Vodă
Dragomirești
VIȘEU DE SUS
BORȘA
Moisei
Recea
14
BAIA MARE
Șișești
Munții Lăpuș
Botiza
Ieud
Băiuț
Săliștea de Sus
Săcel
Pasul Șetref 817
Pietrosul 2302
52
Prislop 1416
Ineu 2279
Fărcașa
1C
Coltău
Dumbrăvița
Săcălășeni
Remetea Chioarului
Satulung
Bârsău de Sus
Sălsig
Ariniș
Cupșeni
Cernești
Munții Țibleș
Țibleș 1839
Romuli
Munții Rodnei
Mireșu Mare
Șomcuta Mare
43
Copalnic-Mănăștur
Lăpuș
17C
Ulmeni
Cehu Silvaniei
Benesat
Valea Chioarului
Vima Mică
TÂRGU LĂPUȘ
Suciu de Sus
42
Telciu
Rodna
73
Năpradea
1C
Boiu Mare
Coroieni
Târlișua
Parva
Maieru
Măgura Ilvei
Letca
Șomeș-Odorhei
29
E 58
Lozna
Ileanda
Poiana Blenchii
Chiuiești
Zagra
Coșbuc
Rebra
SÂNGEORZ-BĂI
Ilva Mică
Salva
Rebrișoara
Leșu
Ilva Mare
Băbeni
1H
E 671
43
Gâlgău
Ciceu-Giurgești
Spermezeu
NĂSĂUD
17D
Feldru
Heniul Mare 1610
M. Bârgăului
JIBOU
Surduc
Rus
Căianu Mic
Chiuza
Nimigea de Jos
Someșul Mare
Prundu Bârgăului
Tiha Bârgăului
4
Cristolț
Zalha
Vad
Câtcău
Cășeiu
Reteag
23
Uriu
BECLEAN
20
Dumitra
Livezile
Creaca
Gârbou
Bobâlna
Cuzdrioara
E 58
DEJ
Șintereag
25
17C
Josenii Bârgăului
Bistrița Bârgăului
19
Bălan
1G
Șieu-Odorhei
17
Mica
Unguraș
E 576
Șieu
BISTRIȚA
Jichișu de Jos
Măgheruș
Budacu de Jos
Satu Nou
Munții
Poiana
24
13
Hida
Recea-Cristur
Cornești
1C
Mintiu Gherlii
Nușeni
Lechința
Dragu
Panticeu
GHERLA
Fizeșu Gherlii
Sânmărtin
Mărișelu
Șieu
Zimbor
Alunis
Iclod
Galații Bistriței
Șieuț
Vătava
E 81
1F
48
Aschileu Mare
Vultureni
Dăbâca
Matei
Chiochiș
Sânmihaiu de Câmpie
47
15A
Monor
Deda
Rușii-Munți
Borșa
44
Sic
Țaga
Buza
Budești
Teaca
Alunis
Aghireșu
Bonțida
Nadăș
Sânpaul
Chinteni
E 576
Jucu de Sus
Pălatca
Geaca
Miceștii de Câmpie
E 576
Batoș
Brâncovenești
Gârbău
E 81
13
Apahida
91
Mociu
Cătina
Lunca
Silivașu de Câmpie
Milaș
Cozma
Suseni
Ideciu de Jos
Baciu
1
1F
Căpușu Mare
Gilău
Florești
CLUJ-NAPOCA
Căianu
16
Cămărașu
Fărăgău
REGHIN
Solovăstru
Someșu Mic
Cojocna
Sărmașu
Urmeniș
Crăiești
16
Breaza
Gurghiu
Beica de Jos
Feleacu
Frata
Mihesu de Câmpie
Răciu
Volvodeni
Petelea
22
Măguri-Răcătău
Săvădisla
E 60
Aiton
Ceanu Mare
Bala
Gornești
Chibed
Ciurila
E 81
Ploscoș
Pogăceaua
Glodeni
20
26
Valea Ierii
Tureni
Valea Largă
Zau de Câmpie
Șăulia
Șincai
Ceuașu de Câmpie
Hodoșa
1
TURDA
Tritenii de Jos
Taureni
Grebenișu de Câmpie
Sâncraiu de Mureș
Ernei
Vărgata
Băișoara
Iara
Petreștii de Jos
Viișoara
Band
12
Sângeorgiu de Mureș
Măgherani
1824
Mihai Viteazu
E 60
CÂMPIA TURZII
Sânger
Pănet
Cristești
TÂRGU MUREȘ
Miercurea Nirajului
Poșaga de Jos
Ocoliș
75
32
Luna
LUDUȘ
Iclănzel
Ungheni
14
Gălești
Baia de Arieș
Moldovenești
1
45
Lunca Mureșului
15
15
Iernut
Acățari
Neaua
13A
P. Secuiului 1129
84
Rimetea
E 81
Chețani
Cuci
Bogata
Ogra
Sânpaul
Gheorghe Doja
24
Fântânele
Sângeorgiu de Pădure
Sălciua
Unirea
Noslac
Ațintiș
Cucerdea
33
Coroisânmartin
Mirăslău
Bichiș
14A
Mica
Suplac
Bălăușeri
Ponor
Livezile
OCNA MUREȘ
16
Bahnea
Zagăr
34
Vețca
Sâcel
Munții Trascăului
AIUD
Râmeț
Hopârta
Fărău
TÂRNĂVENI
Gănești
Nadeș
Mogoș
Lopadea Nouă
Adămuș
39
14A
Băgaciu
Viișoara
Secuieni
13
Întregalde
Stremț
Rădești
Jidvei
Cetatea de Baltă
SIGHIȘOARA
1
Sâncel
Dumbrăveni
Hoghilag
Cricău
Teiuș
Crăciunelu de Jos
Șona
25
Blăjel
Dârlos
14
Daneș
Albești
14B
38
Laslea
Galda de Jos
Mihalț
24
Bazna
Ighiu
16
BLAJ
Valea Lungă
Târnava
Brateiu
Metes
74
Sântimbru
Copșa Mică
MEDIAȘ
Ațel
Biertan
Apold
E 81
Berghin
Cergău Mare
28
Micăsasa
Moșna
ALBA IULIA
Cenade
14B
Axente Sever
Valea Viilor
29
Iacobeni
Brădeni
Ciugud
Ohaba
Rosia de Secaș
Șeica Mică
Blandiana
Daia Română
Păuca
Șeica Mare
Bârghiș
41
Vințu de Jos
17
SEBEȘ
Mihăileni
AGNITA
Șpring
Doștat
Loamneș
55
Merghindeal
Șibot
E 68
Pianu de Sus
Cut
Miercurea Sibiului
Ludoș
Vurpăr
Altina
7
Câlnic
Apoldu
Slimnic
52
Chirpăr
Cincu
32
Șoarș

83
90

C
D
ČERNIVCI
NOVOSELYCA
STOROŽYNEC
Hlyboka
Herca
Berehomet
Vyznycja
Lopušna
Krasnoil's'k
Vicovu de Sus
Siret
DOROHOI
DARABANI
RĂDĂUȚI
Milișăuți
BOTOȘANI
Solca
Cajvana
SUCEAVA
Salcea
GURA HUMORULUI
CÂMPULUNG MOLDOVENESC
FĂLTICENI
Liteni
Dolhasca
VATRA-DORNEI
Broșteni
PAȘCANI
TÂRGU-NEAMȚ
Bicaz
PIATRA-NEAMȚ
Roznov
Buhuși
TOPLIȚA
Borsec
GHEORGHENI
Bălan
MOINEȘTI
COMĂNEȘTI
DĂRMĂNEȘTI
TÂRGU OCNA
MIERCUREA-CIUC
ODORHEIU SECUIESC
Vlăhița
Băile Tușnad
Slănic-Moldova
Baraolt
TÂRGU SECUIESC
Obcina Mare
Ob. Feredeului
Ob. Mestecăniș
Munții Stânișoarei
Munții Bistriței
M-ții Ceahlău
Munții Giurgeului
M-ții Tarcăului
M-ții Goșmanu
Munții Gurghiului
Munții Harghita
M-ții Ciucului
Munții Nemirei
M-ții Bodocului
M-ții Baraoltului
Munții Vrancei
Călimani
Suceava
Moldova
Siret
Bistrița
L. Izvorul Muntelui
Olt
E 85
E 576
E 578
E 574
E 58

1

2

86

3

4

91

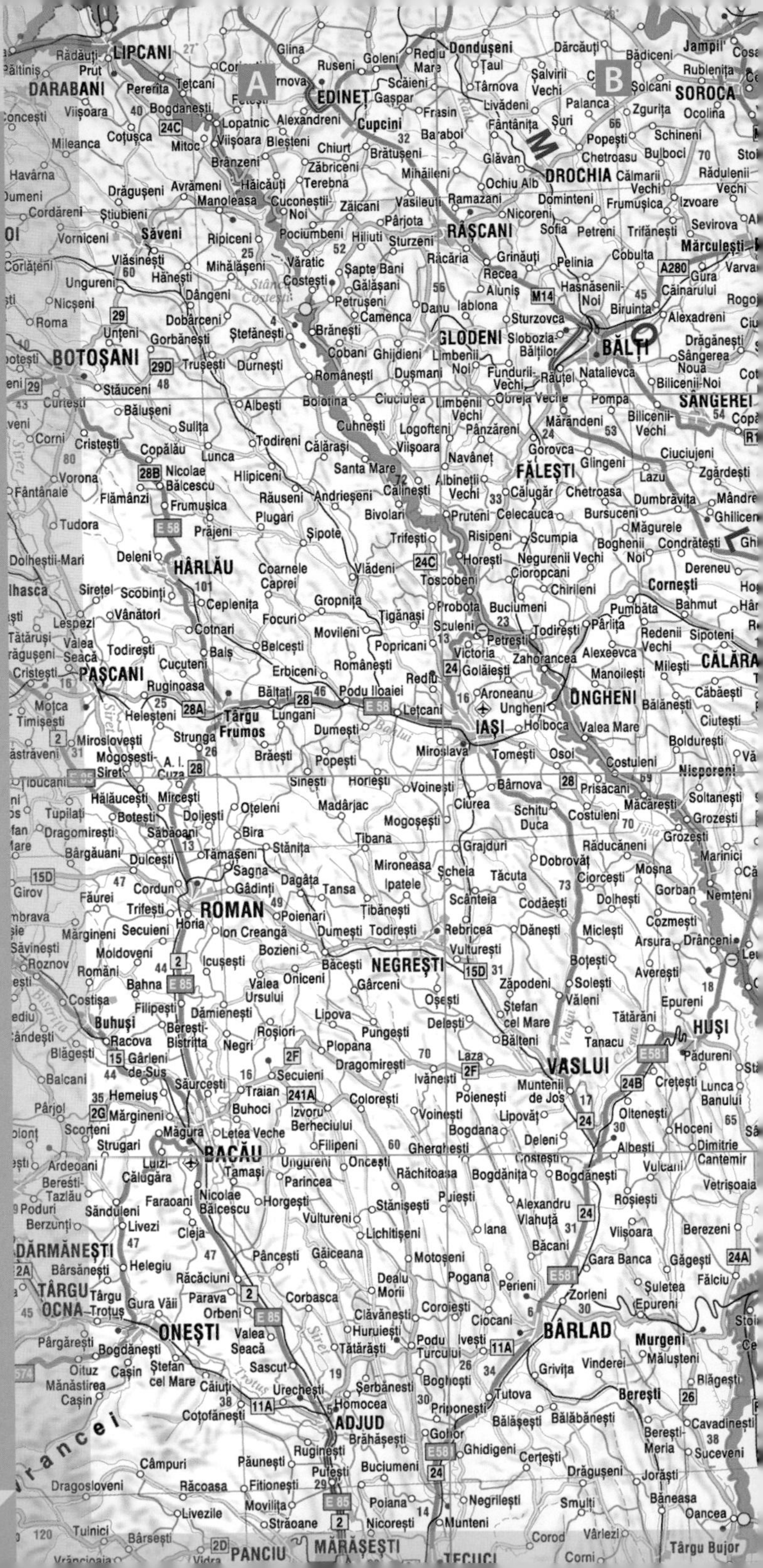

A B C

1 2 3 4

Rădăuţi-Prut, LIPCANI, Păltiniş, DARABANI, Pererita, Teţcani, Corjeuţi, Glina, Trinca, Ruseni, Goleni, Rediu Mare, Donduşeni, Dărcăuţi, Bădiceni, Jampil', Cosăuţi, Rubleniţa, Şolcani, SOROCA, Ocolina, Ţaul, Scăieni, Târnova, Şalvirii Vechi, Palanca, Zguriţa, EDINEŢ, Gaşpar, Frasin, Livădeni, Fântâniţa, Şuri, Popeşti, Schineni, Bulboci, Stoicani, Conceşti, Viişoara, Bogdaneşti, Lopatnic, Alexăndreni, Cupcini, Baraboi, Chetroasu, Rădulenii Vechi, Mileanca, Coţuşca, Mitoc, Viişoara, Bleşteni, Chiurt, Brătuşeni, Glăvan, DROCHIA, Călmarii Vechi, Havârna, Brânzeni, Zăbriceni, Mihăileni, Ochiu Alb, Izvoare, Dumeni, Drăguşeni, Avrămeni, Hăicăuţi, Terebna, Ramazani, Dominteni, Frumuşica, Cordăreni, Ştiubieni, Manoleasa, Cuconeştii-Noi, Zăicani, Vasileuţi, Nicoreni, Pârjota, RÂŞCANI, Sofia, Petreni, Trifăneşti, Sevirova, Vorniceni, Săveni, Ripiceni, Pociumbeni, Hiliuţi, Sturzeni, Mărculeşti, Corlăţeni, Vlăsineşti, Mihălăşeni, Văratic, Răcăria, Grinăuţi, Pelinia, Cobulta, Varvareuca, Ungureni, Hăneşti, Costeşti, Şapte Bani, Recea, Gălăşeni, Aluniş, Hasnăşenii-Noi, Gura Căinarului, Nicşeni, Dângeni, L. Stânca Costeşti, Petruşeni, Danu, Iablona, Biruinţa, Rogojeni, Roma, Dobârceni, Camenca, Sturzovca, Alexandreni, Unţeni, Gorbăneşti, Ştefăneşti, Brăneşti, GLODENI, Slobozia-Bălţilor, BĂLŢI, Drăgăneşti, BOTOŞANI, Truşeşti, Durneşti, Cobani, Ghijdieni, Limbenii Noi, Fundurii-Vechi, Răuţel, Natalievca, Sângerea Nouă, Stăuceni, Româneşti, Duşmani, Bilicenii-Noi, Curteşti, Albeşti, Bolotina, Ciuciulea, Limbenii Vechi, Obreja Veche, Pompa, SÂNGEREI, Băluşeni, Suliţa, Cuhneşti, Logofteni, Pânzăreni, Mărăndeni, Bilicenii-Vechi, Corni, Cristeşti, Todireni, Călăraşi, Viişoara, Gorovca, Copălău, Lunca, Navâneţ, Glingeni, Ciuciujeni, Vorona, Nicolae Bălcescu, Hlipiceni, Santa Mare, Albineţii Vechi, FĂLEŞTI, Lazu, Zgărdeşti, Fântânele, Flămânzi, Frumuşica, Răuseni, Andrieşeni, Călineşti, Călugăr, Chetroasa, Dumbrăviţa, Mândreşti, Plugari, Bivolari, Pruteni, Celecauca, Bursuceni, Ghiliceni, Tudora, Prăjeni, Şipote, Trifeşti, Risipeni, Scumpia, Măgurele, Boghenii Noi, Condrăteşti, Deleni, HÂRLĂU, Coarnele Caprei, Vlădeni, Toscobeni, Horeşti, Negurenii Vechi, Cioropcani, Dereneu, Dolheştii-Mari, Siretel, Scobinţi, Ceplenita, Gropniţa, Ţigănaşi, Probota, Chirileni, Corneşti, Pumbăta, Bahmut, Vânători, Focuri, Buciumeni, Sculeni, Todireşti, Pârliţa, Redenii Vechi, Sipoteni, Lespezi, Cotnari, Movileni, Popricani, Petreşti, Alexeevca, Valea Seacă, Todireşti, Balş, Belceşti, Victoria, Zahorancea, Mileşti, CĂLĂRAŞI, PAŞCANI, Cucuteni, Erbiceni, Româneşti, Golăieşti, Manoileşti, Ruginoasa, Băltaţi, Podu Iloaiei, Rediu, Aroneanu, UNGHENI, Cabăeşti, Moţca, Heleşteni, Târgu Frumos, Lungani, Leţcani, Ungheni, Bălăneşti, Ciuteşti, Timişeşti, Strunga, Dumeşti, IAŞI, Holboca, Valea Mare, Mirosloveşti, Brăeşti, Popeşti, Miroslava, Tomeşti, Osoi, Boldureşti, Mogoşeşti-Siret, A. I. Cuza, Costuleni, Sineşti, Horleşti, Voineşti, Bârnova, Prisăcani, NISPORENI, Hălăuceşti, Mirceşti, Madârjac, Ciurea, Schitu Duca, Costuleni, Măcăreşti, Soltaneşti, Tupilaţi, Boteşti, Doljeşti, Oţeleni, Mogoşeşti, Grozeşti, Dragomireşti, Săbăoani, Bira, Ţibana, Grajduri, Răducăneni, Bârgăuani, Dulceşti, Tămăşeni, Stăniţa, Mironeasa, Şcheia, Dobrovăţ, Ciorceşti, Moşna, Marinici, Sagna, Gâdinţi, Dagâţa, Tansa, Ipatele, Tăcuta, Dolheşti, Gorban, Nemţeni, Girov, Făurei, Cordun, Trifeşti, ROMAN, Poienari, Ţibăneşti, Scânteia, Codăeşti, Cozmeşti, Mărgineni, Secuieni, Horia, Ion Creangă, Dumeşti, Todireşti, Rebricea, Dăneşti, Mircleşti, Arsura, Drânceni, Săvineşti, Moldoveni, Bozieni, Vultureşti, Roznov, Români, Icuşeşti, Băceşti, NEGREŞTI, Boţeşti, Avereşti, Bahna, Valea Ursului, Oniceni, Gârceni, Zăpodeni, Soleşti, Costişa, Filipeşti, Dămieneşti, Oşeşti, Ştefan cel Mare, Văleni, Epureni, Buhuşi, Bereşti-Bistriţa, Lipova, Deleşti, Tătărăni, HUŞI, Racova, Roşiori, Pungeşti, Bălteni, Tanacu, Blăgeşti, Gârleni de Sus, Negri, Plopana, Laza, Pădureni, Secuieni, Dragomireşti, Ivăneşti, VASLUI, Balcani, Săucreşti, Traian, Poieneşti, Munteni de Jos, Creţeşti, Lunca Banului, Hemeiuş, Buhoci, Izvoru Berheciului, Coloreşti, Voineşti, Lipovăţ, Olteneşti, Pârjol, Mărgineni, Bogdana, Hoceni, Scorţeni, Măgura, Letea Veche, Filipeni, Deleni, Albeşti, Dimitrie Cantemir, Strugari, BACĂU, Gherghesti, Ardeoani, Luizi-Călugăra, Tamaşi, Ungureni, Onceşti, Răchitoasa, Bogdăniţa, Costeşti, Bogdăneşti, Vulcani, Bereşti-Tazlău, Parincea, Vetrişoaia, Poduri, Sănduleni, Faraoani, Nicolae Bălcescu, Horgeşti, Stănişeşti, Puieşti, Alexandru Vlahuţă, Roşieşti, Berzunţi, Livezi, Cleja, Vultureni, Lichitişeni, Iana, Vilşoara, Berezeni, DĂRMĂNEŞTI, Helegiu, Pânceşti, Găiceana, Motoşeni, Băcani, Gara Banca, Găgeşti, Bârsăneşti, Răcăciuni, Dealu Morii, Pogana, Perieni, Fălciu, TÂRGU OCNA, Târgu Trotuş, Gura Văii, Parava, Orbeni, Corbasca, Clăvăneşti, Coroieşti, Zorleni, Şuletea, Epureni, Ciocani, ONEŞTI, Valea Seacă, Huruieşti, BÂRLAD, Murgeni, Pârgăreşti, Bogdăneşti, Tătărăşti, Podu Turcului, Iveşti, Mălusteni, Oituz, Caşin, Ştefan cel Mare, Sascut, Grivita, Vinderei, Mănăstirea Caşin, Căiuţi, Urecheşti, Şerbăneşti, Boghesti, Tutova, Bereşti, Blăgeşti, Cotofăneşti, Homocea, Priponeşti, Bălăşeşti, Bălăbăneşti, Cavadineşti, ADJUD, Brăhăşeşti, Gohor, Bereşti-Meria, Câmpuri, Păuneşti, Ruginesti, Buciumeni, Ghidigeni, Cerţeşti, Suceveni, Dragosloveni, Răcoasa, Puteşti, Fitioneşti, Drăguşeni, Jorăşti, Livezile, Moviliţa, Poiana, Negrileşti, Smulţi, Băneasa, Oancea, Tulnici, Bârseşti, Străoane, Nicoreşti, Munteni, Corod, Vârlezi, Vrâncioaia, Vidra, PANCIU, MĂRĂŞEŞTI, TECUCI, Corni, Târgu Bujor

Prut, Siret, Bahlui, Jijia, Bistriţa, Trotuş, Vaslui, Crasna, Răut, Vrancei

M14, A280, 24C, 29, 29D, 28B, E 58, 28, 28A, 2, E 85, 24, 15D, 2F, 241A, 2G, 15, 2A, 11A, E 581, 24B, 24A, 26, 2D

85

92

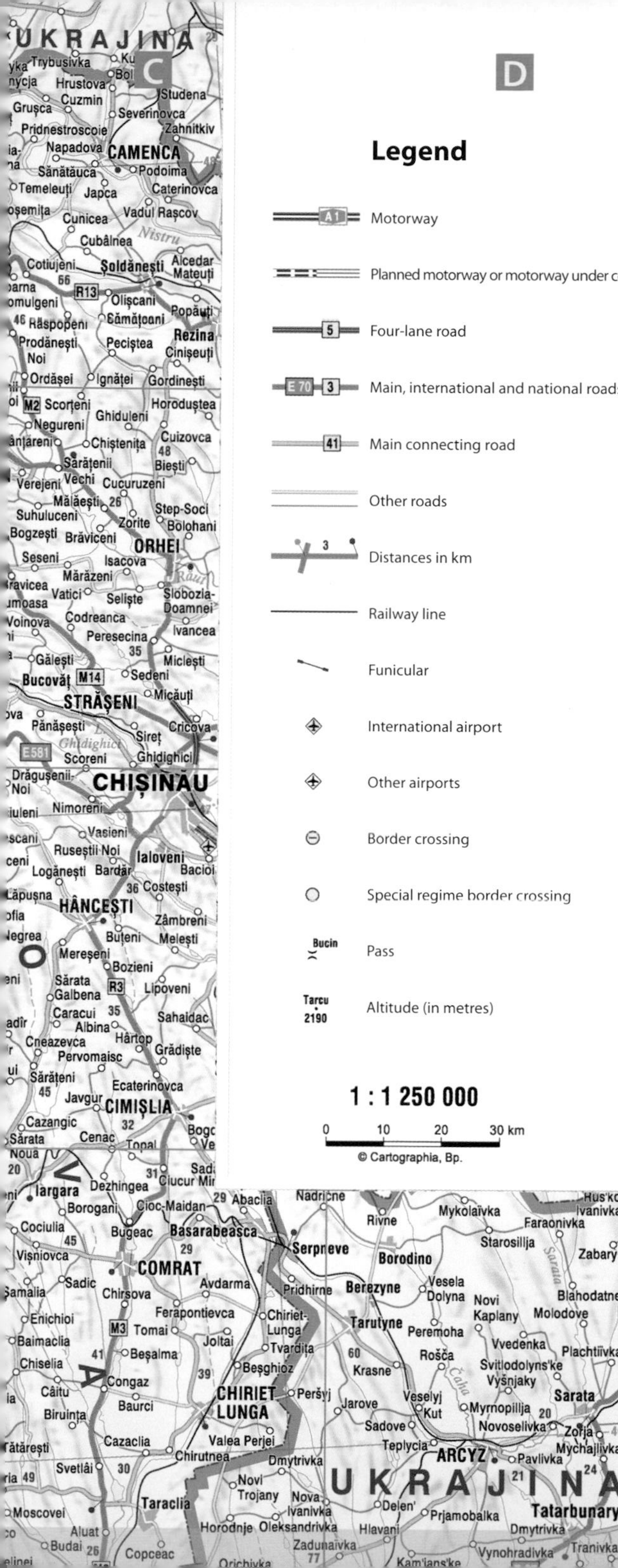

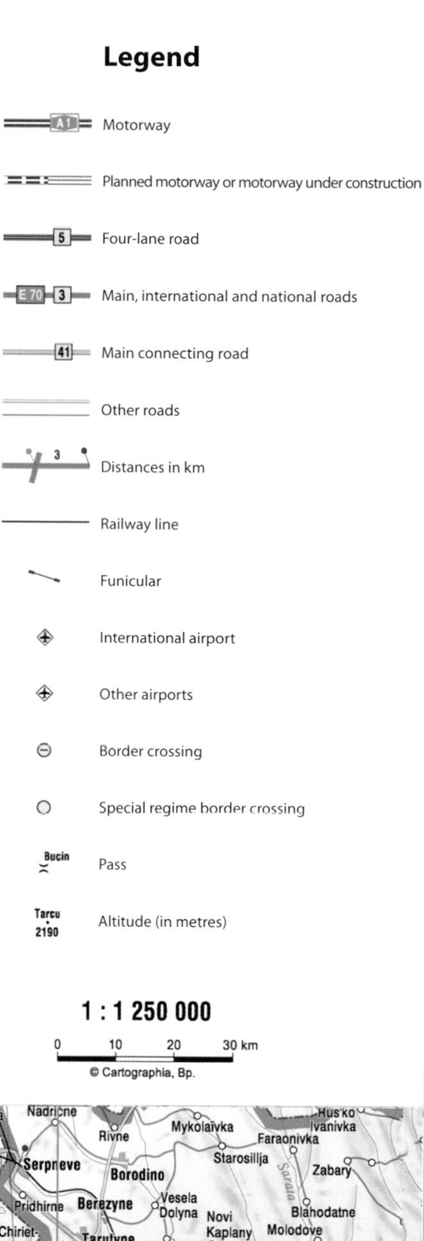

D

Legend

- Motorway
- Planned motorway or motorway under construction
- Four-lane road
- Main, international and national roads
- Main connecting road
- Other roads
- Distances in km
- Railway line
- Funicular
- International airport
- Other airports
- Border crossing
- Special regime border crossing
- Pass
- Altitude (in metres)

1 : 1 250 000

0 10 20 30 km

© Cartographia, Bp.

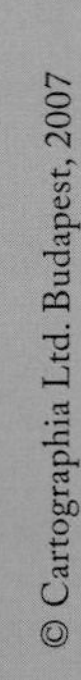

93

82

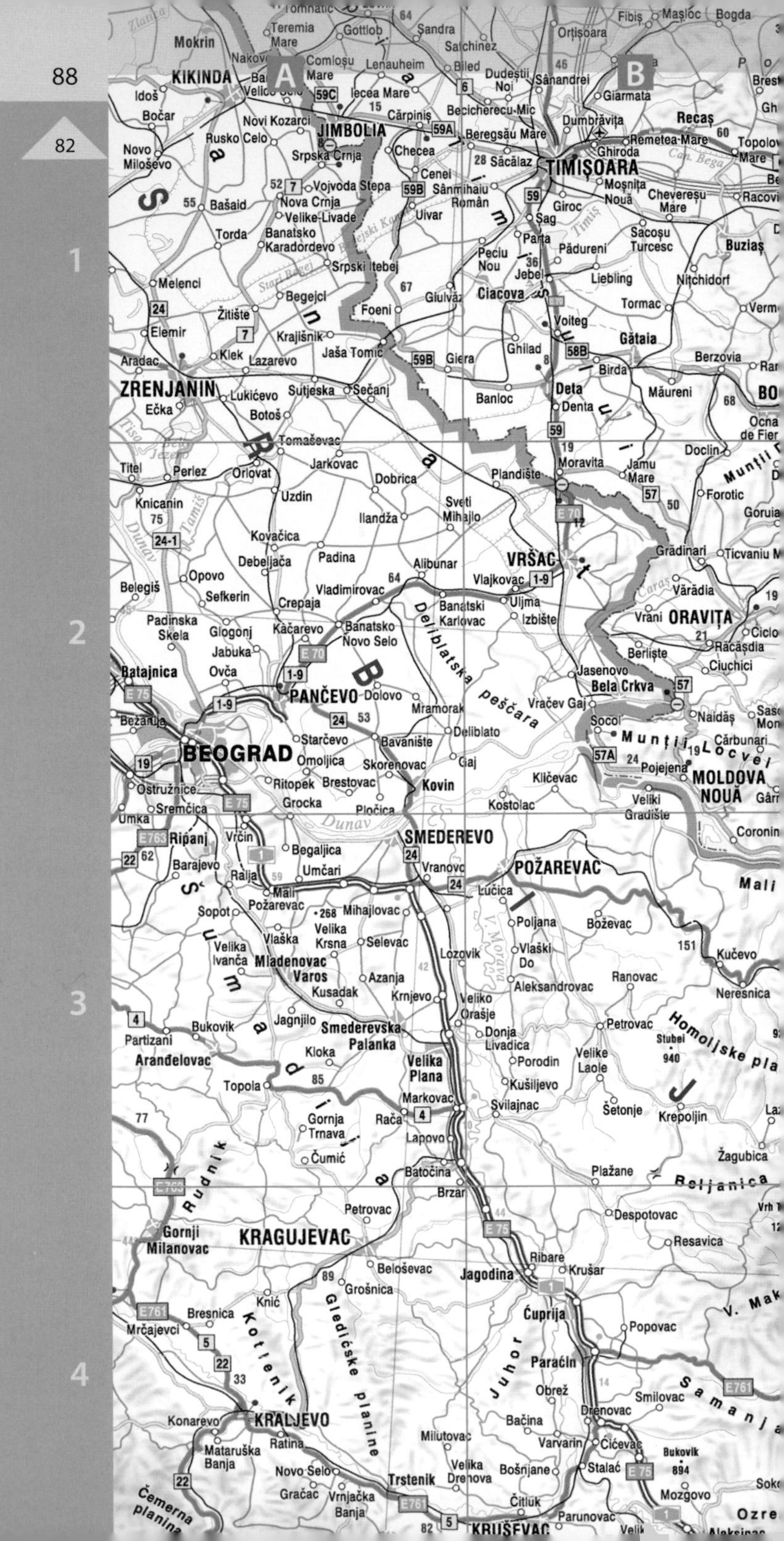
A
B
1
2
3
4
Mokrin
KIKINDA
Idoš
Bočar
Novo Miloševo
Rusko Selo
Novi Kozarci
JIMBOLIA
Srpska Crnja
Teremia Mare
Gottlob
Comloşu Mare
Lenauheim
Iecea Mare
Cărpiniş
Checea
Sandra
Satchinez
Biled
Dudeştii Noi
Becicherecu Mic
Beregsău Mare
Săcălaz
Cenei
Sânmihaiu Român
Uivar
Orţişoara
Sânandrei
Giarmata
Dumbrăviţa
Ghiroda
TIMIŞOARA
Recaş
Remetea Mare
Moşniţa Nouă
Chevereşu Mare
Giroc
Şag
Parţa
Pădureni
Sacoşu Turcesc
Buziaş
Peciu Nou
Jebel
Liebling
Nitchidorf
Ciacova
Tormac
Voiteg
Găiaia
Ghilad
Birda
Berzovia
Deta
Denta
Măureni
Banloc
Giera
Foeni
Giulvăz
Vojvoda Stepa
Nova Crnja
Velike Livade
Bašaid
Torda
Banatsko Karađorđevo
Srpski Itebej
Begejci
Melenci
Žitište
Elemir
Krajišnik
Jaša Tomić
Klek
Lazarevo
Aradac
ZRENJANIN
Lukićevo
Sutjeska
Sečanj
Ečka
Botoš
Tomaševac
Jarkovac
Dobrica
Titel
Perlez
Orlovat
Knićanin
Uzdin
Ilandža
Sveti Mihajlo
Plandište
Moravita
Jamu Mare
Doclin
Forotic
Kovačica
Padina
Debeljača
Alibunar
VRŠAC
Vlajkovac
Grădinari
Opovo
Sefkerin
Belegiš
Vladimirovac
Banatski Karlovac
Uljma
Izbište
Crepaja
Padinska Skela
Glogonj
Kačarevo
Banatsko Novo Selo
Jabuka
Ovča
Batajnica
Deliblatska peščara
Oraviţa
Vrani
Berlişte
Răcăşdia
Ciuchici
Jasenovo
Bela Crkva
Vračev Gaj
PANČEVO
Dolovo
Mramorak
Bežanija
BEOGRAD
Starčevo
Omoljica
Bavanište
Deliblato
Gaj
Socol
Naidăş
Munţii Locvei
Pojejena
MOLDOVA NOUĂ
Ritopek
Brestovac
Skorenovac
Kovin
Kličevac
Ostružnica
Sremčica
Grocka
Umka
Ripanj
Vrčin
Dunav
Ploćica
Kostolac
Veliki Gradište
SMEDEREVO
Begaljica
Umčari
Vranovo
POŽAREVAC
Barajevo
Ralja
Mali Požarevac
Lučica
Sopot
Mihajlovac
Poljana
Boževac
Vlaška
Velika Krsna
Selevac
Velika Ivanča
Mladenovac Varoš
Lozovik
Vlaški Do
Kučevo
Azanja
Kusadak
Krnjevo
Aleksandrovac
Ranovac
Neresnica
Veliko Orašje
Partizani
Bukovik
Jagnjilo
Smederevska Palanka
Donja Livadica
Petrovac
Homoljske planine
Aranđelovac
Kloka
Velika Plana
Porodin
Velike Laole
Kušiljevo
Topola
Markovac
Svilajnac
Šetonje
Krepoljin
Gornja Trnava
Rača
Lapovo
Čumić
Batočina
Žagubica
Rudnik
Brzan
Plažane
Beljanica
Petrovac
Despotovac
Gornji Milanovac
KRAGUJEVAC
Resavica
Ribare
Beloševac
Jagodina
Krušar
Grošnica
Knić
Ćuprija
Bresnica
Mrčajevci
Popovac
Kotlenik
Gledićske planine
Juhor
Paraćin
Obrež
Samanja
Smilovac
Drenovac
Konarevo
KRALJEVO
Bačina
Mataruška Banja
Ratina
Milutovac
Varvarin
Ćićevac
Novo Selo
Velika Drenova
Bošnjane
Stalać
Gračac
Vrnjačka Banja
Trstenik
Čitluk
Mozgovo
Čemerna planina
Parunovac
KRUŠEVAC
E 70
E 75
E 761
E 763
59C
59A
59B
59
58B
57
57A
24
24-1
1-9
19
22
7
6
5
4
1

83

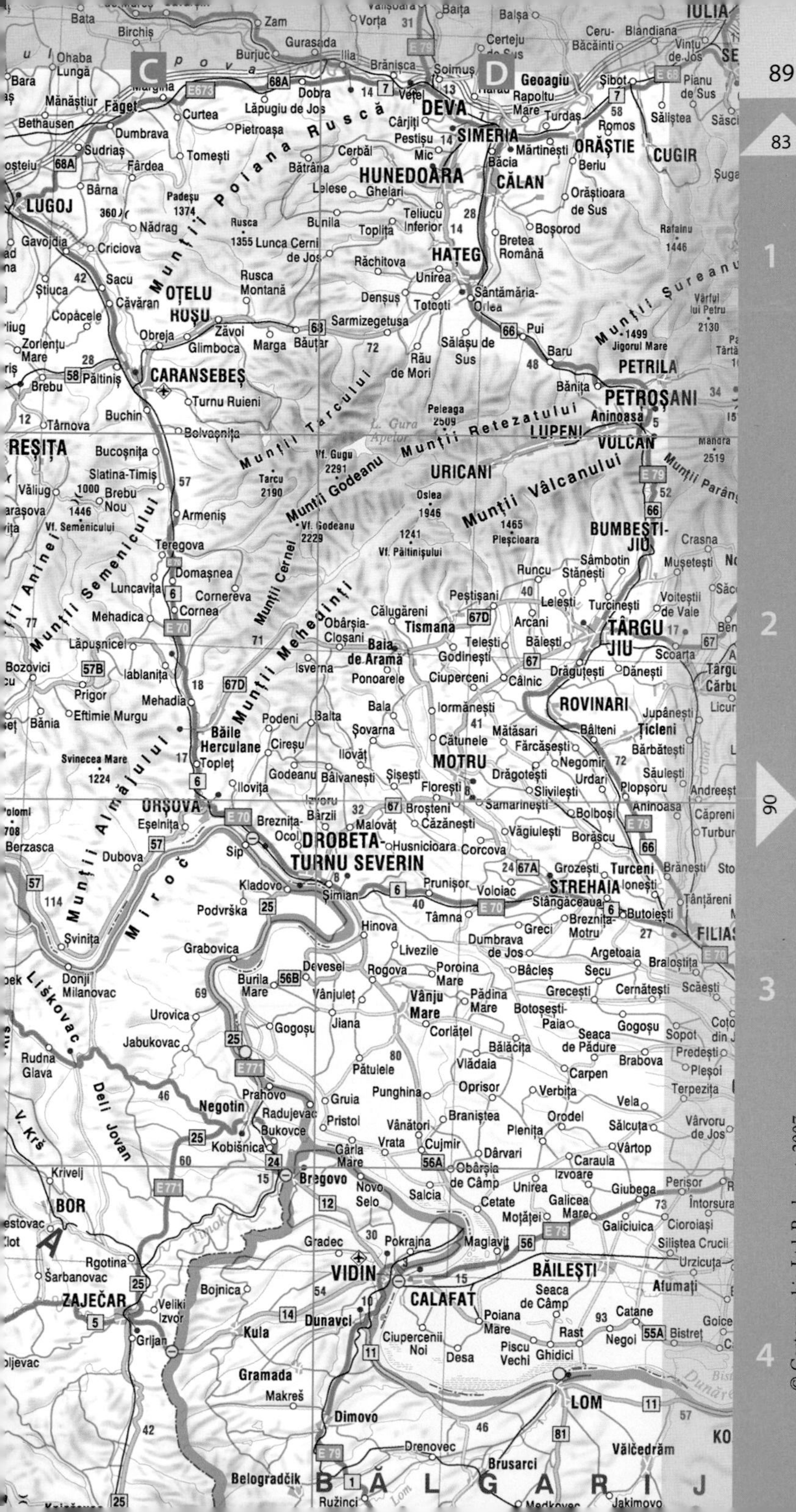
C
D
A
Munții Poiana Ruscă
Munții Țarcului
Munții Godeanu
Munții Retezatului
Munții Vâlcanului
Munții Parâng
Munții Șureanu
Munții Cernei
Munții Mehedinți
Munții Semenicului
Munții Aninei
Munții Almăjului
Miroč
Deli Jovan
Liškovac
DEVA
SIMERIA
HUNEDOARA
CĂLAN
ORĂȘTIE
CUGIR
Geoagiu
HAȚEG
LUGOJ
Făget
OȚELU ROȘU
CARANSEBEȘ
REȘIȚA
PETRILA
PETROȘANI
LUPENI
VULCAN
URICANI
BUMBEȘTI-JIU
TÂRGU JIU
ROVINARI
Țicleni
MOTRU
Tismana
Baia de Aramă
Băile Herculane
ORȘOVA
DROBETA-TURNU SEVERIN
STREHAIA
Turceni
FILIAȘI
Vânju Mare
Negotin
BOR
ZAJEČAR
VIDIN
CALAFAT
BĂILEȘTI
Dunavci
Kula
Gramada
Dimovo
Belogradčik
LOM
Vâlcedrăm
Brusarci
Bregovo
Novo Selo
Kladovo
Sip
Donji Milanovac
Dubova
Svinița
Peleaga 2509
Vf. Gugu 2291
Țarcu 2190
Vf. Godeanu 2229
Oslea 1946
Mândra 2519
L. Gura Apelor
Dunăre
Timok
BĂLGARIJ

90

84

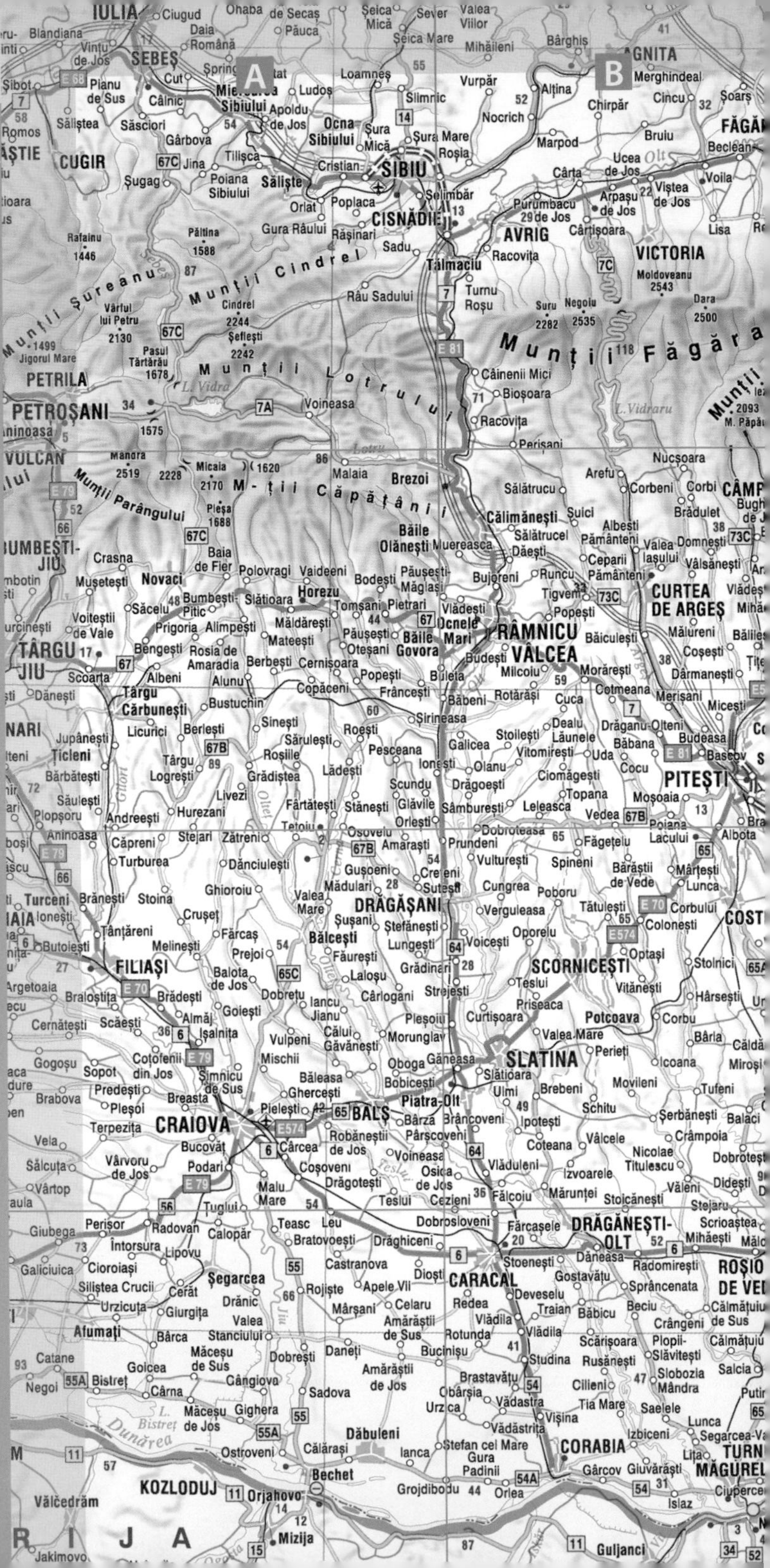

A B

IULIA Ciugud Ohaba de Secaş Şeica Mică Sever Valea Viilor
Blandiana Daia Română Păuca Şeica Mare Mihăileni Bârghiş AGNITA
Vinţu de Jos SEBEŞ Loamneş Merghindeal
Şibot Pianu de Sus Cut Miercurea Sibiului Ludoş Vurpăr Alţina Chirpăr Cincu Şoarş
Romos Sălıştea Câlnic Săsciori Apoldu de Jos Slimnic Nocrich FĂGĂR
ORĂŞTIE CUGIR Gârbova Ocna Sibiului Şura Mică Şura Mare Marpod Bruiu Beclean
Jina Tilişca Cristian SIBIU Roşia Ucea de Jos Olt
Şugag Poiana Sibiului Sălişte Cârţa Voila
Orlat Poplaca Şelimbăr Purumbacu de Jos Arpaşu de Jos Viştea de Jos
Gura Râului Răşinari CISNĂDIE AVRIG Cârţişoara Lisa
Rafainu 1446 Păltina 1588 Sadu Racoviţa VICTORIA
Munţii Cindrel Tălmaciu Turnu Roşu Moldoveanu 2543
Munţii Şureanu Vârful lui Petru 2130 Cindrel 2244 Râu Sadului Suru 2282 Negoiu 2535 Dara 2500
1499 Jigorul Mare Şerbeşti 2242
Pasul Tărtărău 1678 Munţii Lotrului Munţii Făgăraş
PETRILA L. Vidra Câinenii Mici
PETROŞANI Voineasa Bioşoara
Aninoasa 1575 Racoviţa L. Vidraru M. Păpău 2093
VULCAN Mandra 2519 2228 Micaia 2170 1620 Malaia Lotru Perişani Nucşoara
Munţii Parângului M-ţii Căpăţânii Brezoi Sălătrucu Arefu Corbeni Corbi CÂMP
Pleşa 1688 Băile Olăneşti Călimăneşti Suici Albeşti Brădulet Bughea de Jos
BUMBEŞTI-JIU Crasna Baia de Fier Muereasca Sălătrucel Daeşti Pământeni Valea Iaşului Domneşti Vâlsăneşti
Muşeteşti Novaci Polovragi Vaideeni Bodeşti Păuşeşti-Măglaşi Bujoreni Runcu Ceparii Pământeni
Săcelu Bumbeşti-Pitic Slătioara Horezu Tomşani Pietrari Vlădeşti Tigveni CURTEA DE ARGEŞ
Voiteştii de Vale Prigoria Alimpeşti Măldăreşti Păuşeşti Ocnele Mari RÂMNICU VÂLCEA Popeşti Mălureni
TÂRGU JIU Bengeşti Rosia de Amaradia Mateeşti Oteşani Băile Govora Budeşti Băiculeşti Coşeşti
Scoarţa Albeni Berbeşti Cernişoara Alunu Popeşti Buleta Milcoiu Morăreşti Dârmăneşti
Dăneşti Târgu Cărbuneşti Copăceni Frânceşti Băbeni Rotărăşi Cuca Cotmeana Merişani Miceşti
Bustuchin Şirineasa Dealu Lăunele Drăganu-Olteni Budeasa
Jupâneşti Licurici Berleşti Sineşti Roeşti Galicea Stoileşti Vitomireşti Uda Băbana
Ţicleni Sărulesti Pesceana Ioneşti Olanu Cocu PITEŞTI
Bărbăteşti Târgu Logreşti Roşiile Lădeşti Scundu Drăgoeşti Ciomăgeşti
Săuleşti Grădiştea Livezi Olteţ Topana Moşoaia
Plopşoru Andreeşti Hurezani Fărtăţeşti Stăneşti Glăvile Sâmbureşti Leleasca Vedea Poiana Lacului
Aninoasa Stejari Zătreni Tetoiu Osoveiu Orleşti Dobroteasa Albota
Căpreni Amaraşti Prundeni Făgeţelu
Turburea Dănciuleşti Guşoeni Creţeni Vultureşti Spineni Bărăştii de Vede Mârţeşti
Ghioroiu Valea Mare Mădulari Suteşti Cungrea Poboru Lunca
Turceni Brăneşti Stoina DRĂGĂŞANI Tătuleşti Corbului COST
Ioneşti Cruşeţ Şuşani Ştefăneşti Verguleasa Coloneşti
Ţânţăreni Fărcaş Bălceşti Lungeşti Voiceşti Oporelu
Butoieşti Melineşti Prejoi Făureşti Optaşi
FILIAŞI Grădinari SCORNICEŞTI Stolnici
Argetoaia Balota de Jos Laloşu Teslui Vităneşti
Bralostiţa Brădeşti Dobreţu Iancu Jianu Cârlogani Strejeşti Priseaca Hârseşti
Cernăteşti Scăeşti Almăj Goieşti Pleşoiu Curtişoara Potcoava Corbu
Işalniţa Vulpeni Călui Găvăneşti Morunglav Valea Mare Bârla Căldă
Gogoşu Coţofenii din Jos Mischii Oboga Găneasa SLATINA Perieţi Icoana Miroşi
Sopot Predeşti Şimnicu de Sus Băleasa Bobiceşti Slătioara Movileni Tufeni
Brabova Pleşoi Breasta Gherceşti Piatra-Olt Ulmi Brebeni Schitu
Terpeziţa CRAIOVA Pieleşti BALŞ Bârza Brâncoveni Ipoteşti Şerbăneşti Balaci
Vela Bucovăţ Robăneştii de Jos Pârşcoveni Coteanu Vâlcele Crâmpoia
Sălcuţa Vârvoru de Jos Podari Cârcea Voineasa Osica de Jos Izvoarele Nicolae Titulescu Dobroteşti
Vârtop Coşoveni Drăgoteşti Vlăduleni Mărunţei Văleni Dideşti
Malu Mare Teslui Cezieni Fălcoiu Stoicăneşti Stejaru
Giubega Perişor Radovan Tuglui Teasc Leu Dobrosloveni Fărcaşele DRĂGĂNEŞTI-OLT Scrioaştea
Întorsura Calopăr Bratovoeşti Drăghiceni Mihăeşti
Galiciuica Lipovu Castranova Ştoeneşti Dăneasa Radomireşti ROŞIORI DE VEDE
Cioroiaşi Segarcea Rojişte Apele Vii Dioşti CARACAL Gostavăţu Sprâncenata
Siliştea Crucii Cerăt Drănic Celaru Deveselu Traian Beciu Călmăţuiu de Sus
Urzicuţa Giurgiţa Valea Stanciului Mârşani Amărăştii de Sus Redea Vlădila Băbicu Crângeni
Afumaţi Bârca Daneţi Rotunda Scărişoara Plopii-Slăviteşti Călmăţuiu
Catane Goicea Măceşu de Sus Dobreşti Bucinişu Studina Rusăneşti Salcia
Negoi Bistreţ Cârna Cângiova Amărăştii de Jos Brastavăţu Cilieni Slobozia Mândra
Sadova Obârşia Vădastra Tia Mare Saelele Putineiu
L. Bistreţ Măceşu de Jos Gighera Urzica Vişina Lunca
Dunărea Ostroveni Călăraşi Dăbuleni Vădăstriţa Izbiceni Segarcea-Vale
Ianca Stefan cel Mare Gura Padinii CORABIA Liţa TURNU MĂGURELE
KOZLODUJ Orjahovo Bechet Grojdibodu Orlea Gârcov Gluvărăşti Ciuperceni
Vălčedrăm Islaz
Mizija Guljanci
Jakimovo
B U L G A R I J A

E 68 7 67C 14 13 7 7C E 81 7A E 79 66 67C 67 73C 67B 67B 65 65C 64 E 70 E 574 6 E 79 65 56 55 6 54 55 55A 55A 11 11 15 54A 54 34 52

89

1 2 3 4

85

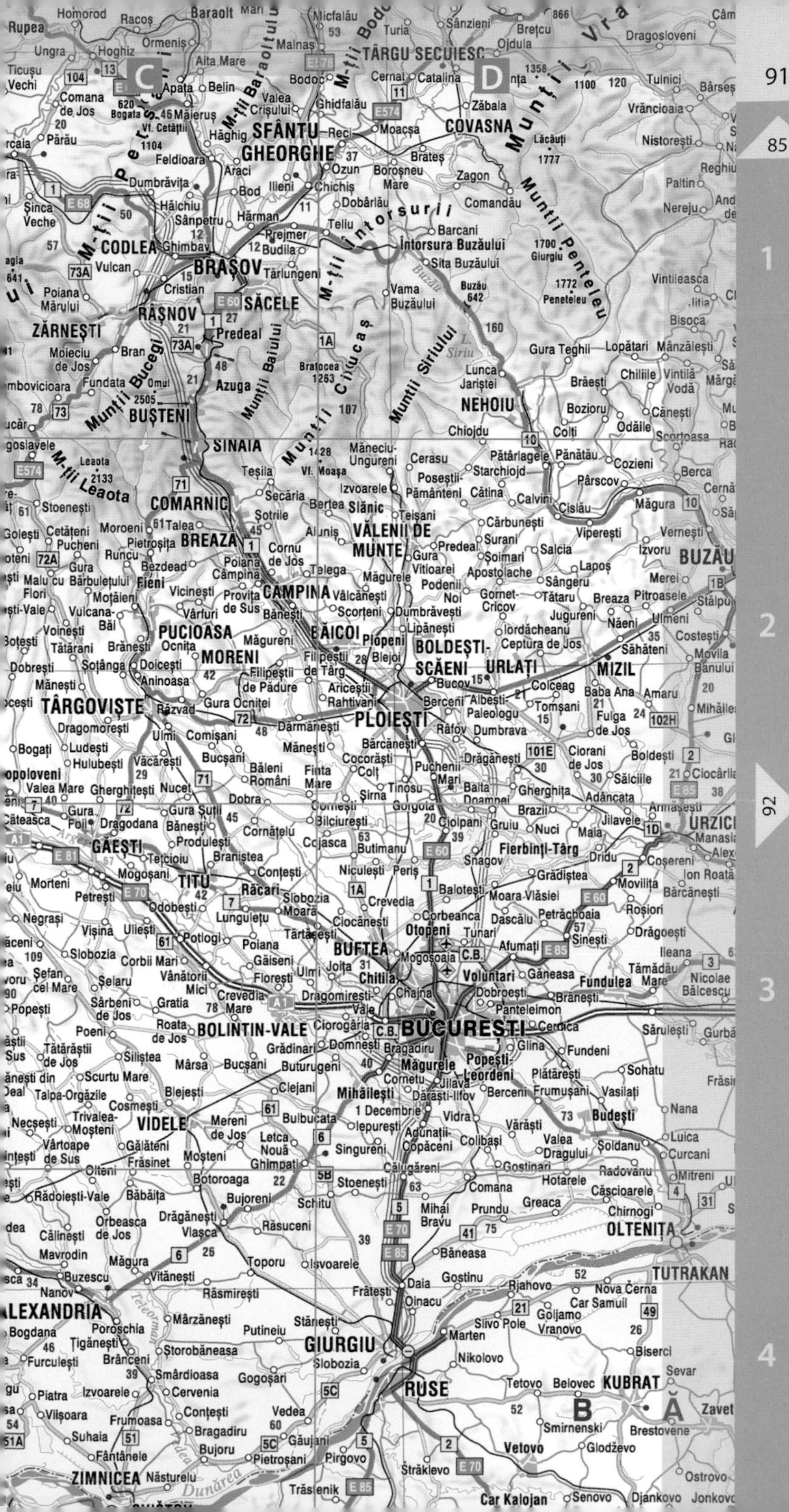
C
D
TÂRGU SECUIESC
SFÂNTU GHEORGHE
COVASNA
CODLEA
BRAȘOV
SĂCELE
RÂȘNOV
ZĂRNEȘTI
Predeal
Azuga
BUȘTENI
SINAIA
COMARNIC
BREAZA
Munții Bucegi
M-ții Leaota
Munții Baiului
Munții Ciucaș
Munții Siriului
M-ții Întorsurii
Întorsura Buzăului
Munții Penteleu
NEHOIU
VĂLENII DE MUNTE
CÂMPINA
BĂICOI
PUCIOASA
MORENI
TÂRGOVIȘTE
PLOIEȘTI
BOLDEȘTI-SCĂENI
URLAȚI
MIZIL
BUZĂU
GĂEȘTI
TITU
Răcari
BUFTEA
Otopeni
Chitila
Voluntari
BUCUREȘTI
BOLINTIN-VALE
Fundulea
Popești-Leordeni
Măgurele
Mihăilești
VIDELE
Budești
OLTENIȚA
TUTRAKAN
ALEXANDRIA
GIURGIU
RUSE
ZIMNICEA
KUBRAT
Vetovo
Dunărea

1
2
3
4

92

86

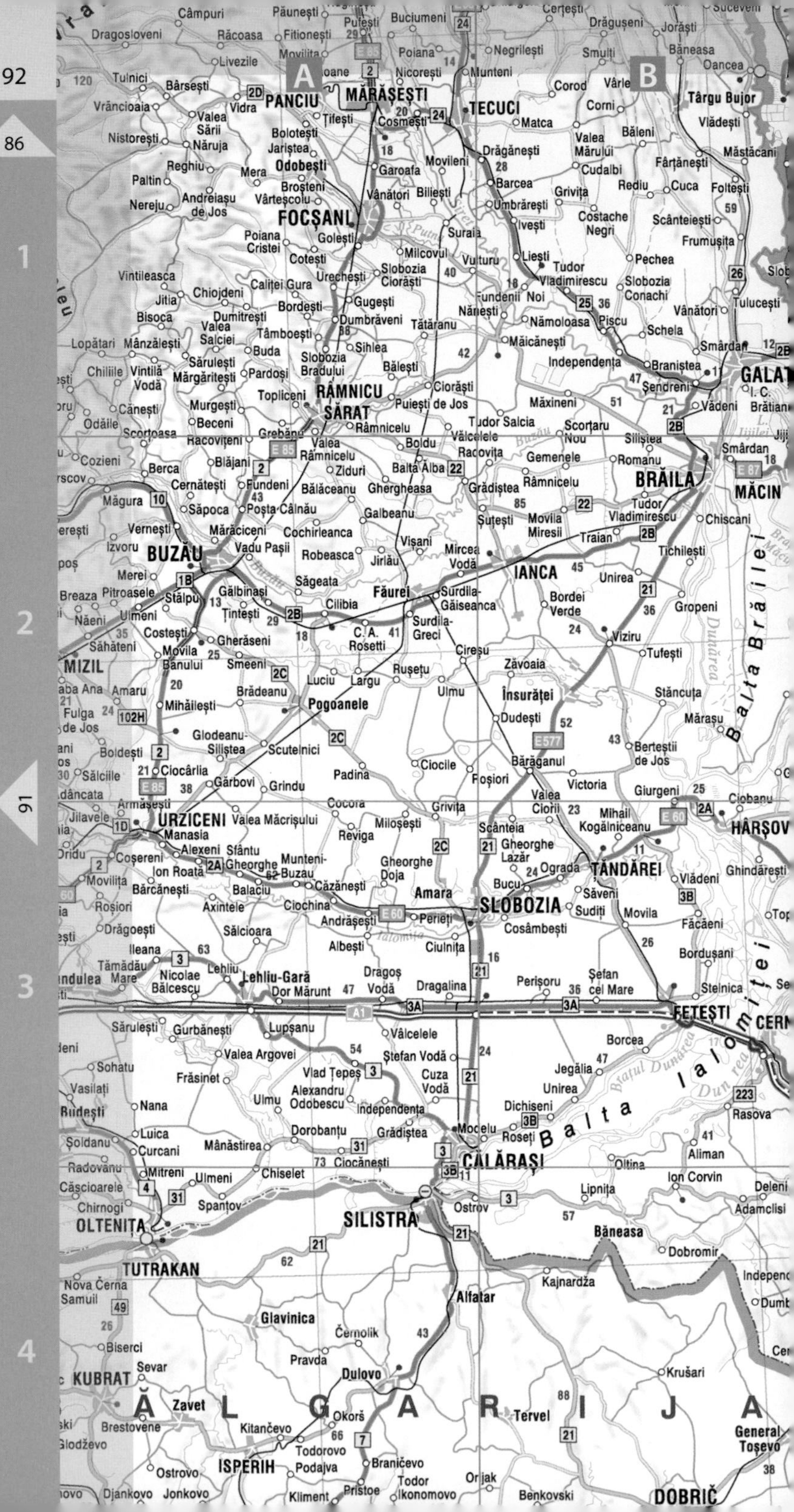
A
B
Câmpuri
Dragosloveni
Răcoasa
Fitionești
Păunești
Pufești
Buciumeni
Cerțești
Drăgușeni
Jorăști
Băneasa
Oancea
Suceveni
Livezile
Poiana
Negrilești
Smulți
Tulnici
Bârsești
PANCIU
MĂRĂȘEȘTI
Nicorești
Munteni
Corod
Vârlezi
Târgu Bujor
Vrâncioaia
Vidra
Valea Sării
Țifești
Cosmești
TECUCI
Matca
Corni
Vlădești
Nistorești
Năruja
Bolotești
Jariștea
Drăgănești
Valea Mărului
Băleni
Măstăcani
Reghiu
Mera
Odobești
Garoafa
Movileni
Barcea
Cudalbi
Fârțănești
Paltin
Broșteni
Vânători
Biliești
Grivița
Rediu
Cuca
Foltești
Nereju
Andreiașu de Jos
Vârteșcoiu
FOCȘANI
Umbrărești
Costache Negri
Scânteiești
Poiana Cristei
Golești
Suraia
Ivești
Frumușița
Cotești
Milcovul
Vulturu
Liești
Tudor Vladimirescu
Pechea
Vintileasca
Urechești
Slobozia Ciorăști
Slobozia Conachi
Jitia
Chiojdeni
Calițe
Gura
Fundenii Noi
Vânători
Tulucești
Bisoca
Dumitrești
Bordești
Gugești
Nănești
Valea Salciei
Dumbrăveni
Tătăranu
Nămoloasa
Piscu
Schela
Lopătari
Mânzălești
Tâmboești
Sihlea
Măicănești
Smârdan
Buda
Independența
Chiliile
Vintilă Vodă
Sărulești
Slobozia Bradului
Bălești
Branistea
GALAȚI
Mărgăritești
Pardoși
Topliceni
RÂMNICU SĂRAT
Ciorăști
Șendreni
Cănești
Murgești
Puiești de Jos
Măxineni
Vădeni
Odăile
Beceni
Râmnicelu
Tudor Salcia
Scorțaru Nou
Scorțoasa
Racovițeni
Grebănu
Valea Râmnicelu
Boldu
Vâlcelele
Siliștea
Cozieni
Blăjani
Ziduri
Racovița
Gemenele
Romanu
Smârdan
Berca
Balta Albă
Grădiștea
Râmnicelu
BRĂILA
MĂCIN
Cernătești
Fundeni
Bălăceanu
Ghergheasa
Măgura
Săpoca
Poșta Câlnău
Galbeanu
Șutești
Movila Miresii
Tudor Vladimirescu
Chiscani
Verneștii
Mărăcineni
Cochirleanca
Vișani
Traian
Izvoru
BUZĂU
Vadu Pașii
Robeasca
Jirlău
Mircea Vodă
IANCA
Tichilești
Merei
Săgeata
Unirea
Breaza
Pitroasele
Gălbinași
Făurei
Surdila-Găiseanca
Bordei Verde
Gropeni
Stâlpu
Cilibia
Năeni
Ulmeni
Țintești
Surdila-Greci
Viziru
Costești
Gherăseni
C. A. Rosetti
Săhăteni
Movila Banului
Smeeni
Cireșu
Tufești
MIZIL
Rușețu
Luciu
Largu
Zăvoaia
Amaru
Brădeanu
Ulmu
Însurăței
Stăncuța
Fulga de Jos
Mihăilești
Pogoanele
Dudești
Mărașu
Glodeanu-Siliștea
Boldești
Scutelnici
Berteștii de Jos
Sălcile
Ciocârlia
Ciocile
Bărăganul
Padina
Victoria
Gârbovi
Grindu
Roșiori
Giurgeni
Ciobanu
Armășești
Cocora
Grivița
Valea Ciorii
Jilavele
URZICENI
Valea Măcrișului
Miloșești
Mihail Kogălniceanu
HÂRȘOVA
Manasia
Reviga
Scânteia
Dridu
Alexeni
Sfântu Gheorghe
Munteni-Buzău
Gheorghe Lazăr
Coșereni
Ion Roată
Gheorghe Doja
Ograda
ȚĂNDĂREI
Ghindărești
Movilița
Bărcănești
Balaciu
Căzănești
Amara
Bucu
Vlădeni
Roșiori
Axintele
Ciochina
Săveni
Andrășești
Perieți
SLOBOZIA
Sudiți
Movila
Drăgoești
Sălcioara
Ialomița
Cosâmbești
Făcăeni
Ileana
Albești
Ciulnița
Bordușani
Tămădău Mare
Nicolae Bălcescu
Lehliu
Lehliu-Gară
Dragoș Vodă
Dor Mărunt
Dragalina
Perișoru
Ștefan cel Mare
Stelnica
FETEȘTI
Sărulești
Gurbănești
Lupșanu
Vâlcelele
Borcea
Valea Argovei
Ștefan Vodă
Sohatu
Vlad Țepeș
Cuza Vodă
Jegălia
Frăsinet
Unirea
Vasilați
Alexandru Odobescu
Nana
Ulmu
Independența
Dichiseni
Budești
Luica
Dorobanțu
Grădiștea
Modelu
Rasova
Șoldanu
Curcani
Mânăstirea
Roseți
Balta Ialomiței
Radovanu
Ciocănești
CĂLĂRAȘI
Aliman
Mitreni
Ulmeni
Chiselet
Oltina
Căscioarele
Ion Corvin
Deleni
Lipnița
Chirnogi
Spanțov
Ostrov
Adamclisi
OLTENIȚA
SILISTRA
Băneasa
TUTRAKAN
Dobromir
Nova Černa
Samuil
Kajnardža
Alfatar
Glavinica
Černolik
Biserci
Sevar
Pravda
Dulovo
Krušari
KUBRAT
Zavet
Tervel
BĂLGARIJA
Brestovene
Kitančevo
Okorš
General Toševo
Glodževo
Todorovo
ISPERIH
Podajva
Braničevo
Ostrovo
Todor Ikonomovo
Orljak
Djankovo
Jonkovo
Kliment
Pristoe
Benkovski
DOBRIČ
Balta Brăilei
Dunărea
Buzău
Putna
Siret
Balta Ialomiței
Brațul Dunărea
E 85
E 60
E 577
E 87
A1

91

87

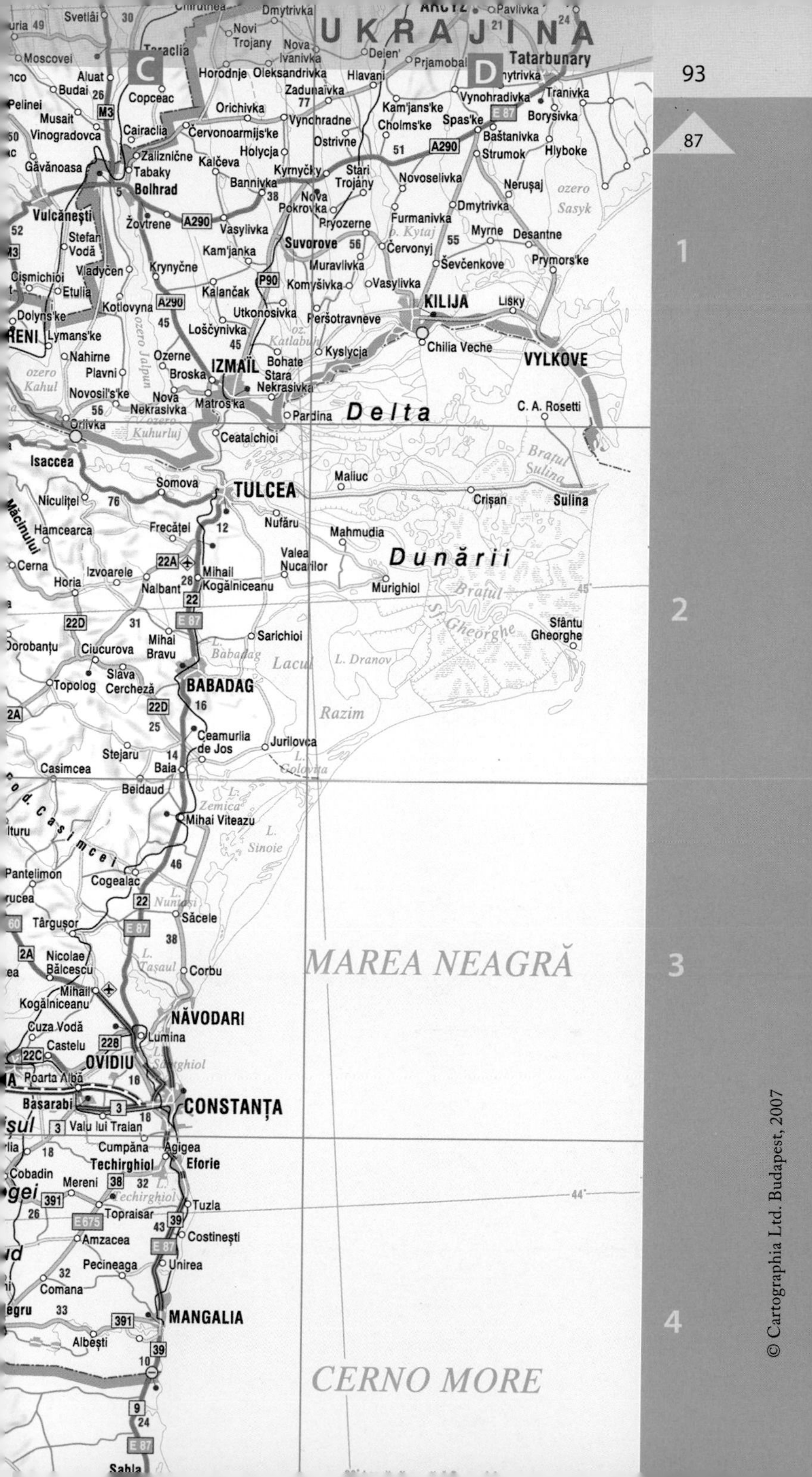
UKRAJINA
C
D
Svetlâi
Dmytrivka
Pavlivka
Novi Trojany
Nova Ivanivka
Delen'
Prjamobal
Tatarbunary
Moscovei
Aluat
Horodnje
Oleksandrivka
Hlavani
Budai
Copceac
Zadunaivka
Vynohradivka
Tranivka
Pelinei
Orichivka
Kam'jans'ke
Musait
Cairaclia
Vynohradne
Cholms'ke
Spas'ke
Borysivka
E 87
Vinogradovca
Červonoarmijs'ke
Ostrivne
Baštanivka
Zaliznične
Holycja
A290
Strumok
Hlyboke
Găvănoasa
Kalčeva
Tabaky
Kyrnyčky
Stari Trojany
Novoselivka
Bolhrad
Bannivka
Nova Pokrovka
Neruşaj
ozero Sasyk
Dmytrivka
Vulcăneşti
Žovtrene
Vasylivka
Pryozerne
Furmanivka
Stefan Vodă
Myrne
Desantne
Kam'janka
Suvorove
ozero Kytaj
Červonyj
Vladyčen
Krynyčne
Muravlivka
Ševčenkove
Prymors'ke
Cişmichioi
P90
Komyšivka
Vasylivka
Etulia
Kalančak
KILIJA
Lisky
Kotlovyna
Utkonosivka
Peršotravneve
Dolyns'ke
Loščynivka
RENI
Lymans'ke
oz. Katlabuh
Chilia Veche
Nahirne
Ozerne
Kyslycja
VYLKOVE
ozero Kahul
Plavni
ozero Jalpuh
IZMAÏL
Broska
Bohate
Stara Nekrasivka
Novosil's'ke
Nova Nekrasivka
Matros'ka
C. A. Rosetti
Pardina
Delta
Orlivka
ozero Kuhurluj
Ceatalchioi
Braţul Sulina
Isaccea
Maliuc
Somova
TULCEA
Crişan
Sulina
Niculiţel
Frecăţei
Nufăru
Mahmudia
Hamcearca
22A
Valea Nucarilor
Dunării
Cerna
Izvoarele
Mihail Kogălniceanu
Murighiol
Horia
Nalbant
Braţul Sf. Gheorghe
22D
E 87
Sfântu Gheorghe
Dorobanţu
Mihai Bravu
Sarichioi
Ciucurova
L. Babadag
L. Dranov
Slava Cercheză
Lacul
Topolog
BABADAG
Razim
Ceamurlia de Jos
Jurilovca
Stejaru
Baia
L. Golovita
Casimcea
Beidaud
L. Zemica
Mihai Viteazu
L. Sinoie
Pantelimon
Cogealac
L. Nuntaşi
Săcele
Târguşor
Nicolae Bălcescu
L. Taşaul
Corbu
MAREA NEAGRĂ
Mihail Kogălniceanu
NĂVODARI
Cuza Vodă
Lumina
Castelu
228
22C
OVIDIU
L. Siutghiol
Poarta Albă
CONSTANŢA
Basarabi
Valu lui Traian
Cumpăna
Agigea
Techirghiol
Eforie
Cobadin
Mereni
L. Techirghiol
Tuzla
391
Topraisar
E675
Costineşti
Amzacea
Pecineaga
Unirea
Comana
MANGALIA
Albeşti
CERNO MORE
Sabla

1

2

3

4

Romania: an unforgettable place

A Romania with the perfumes of the Levant, a Romania that preserves the memory of the "Little Paris", a Romania of churches, a sub-Mediterranean Romania, a Romania of Carpathian peaks... these are just some of the facets this country reveals!

Today's Romania is not a country that can be overlooked – it is a European country in the true sense of the word, a country with its own identity and values, a seductive country, which cannot fail to fascinate. It is a country about which we still have much to learn...